An Operational Guide for Micro-Enterprise Projects

An Operational Guide for Micro-Enterprise Projects

Foreword by Jane Jacobs

ACCION International • The Calmeadow Foundation

Copyright © 1988 by ACCION International/The Calmeadow Foundation
All rights reserved.

Canadian Cataloguing in Publication Data

Main entry under title:
An Operational guide for micro-enterprise projects

ISBN 0-921340-00-1

1. Economic development projects – Developing countries. 2. Community development – Developing countries. 3. Economic assistance – Developing countries. 4. Poor – Developing countries. 5. ACCION International. I. ACCION International. II. Calmeadow Foundation.

HC59.72.E44074 1988   338.91'09172'4   C88-093546-4

Published by
The Calmeadow Foundation
Suite 2000
95 Wellington Street West
Toronto, Ontario M5J 2N7

Editorial and design: Abraham Tanaka Associates
Typesetting: Q Composition Inc.

Printed and bound in Canada

CONTENTS

Foreword by Jane Jacobs ix
Introduction xiii

Chapter 1
The Informal Sector and How It Can Be Assisted 1

THE "INFORMAL ECONOMIC SECTOR" IN
DEVELOPING COUNTRIES 2
   A. Characteristics of informal-sector businesses 2
   B. Importance of informal-sector businesses to the
      local economy 3
ASSISTANCE PROGRAMS THAT WORK 4
   A. Work directly in the community 4
   B. Simplify application procedures 4
   C. Extend credit quickly 4
   D. Do not initially require books and complex
      business plans 5
   E. Do not require guarantees that would eliminate
      most potential candidates 5
   F. Work with existing micro-businesses or help start
      others that are appropriate for the community 5
   G. Focus on the local market 5
   H. Extend small short-term loans primarily for
      working capital 5
   I. Charge interest rates at the market rate or higher ... 5
   J. Allow loan recipients to assume a major role in
      promoting the program 6
TRADITIONAL AND NON-TRADITIONAL
APPROACHES TO MICRO-ENTERPRISE
DEVELOPMENT 6
   A. Clients 7

    B. Outreach 7
    C. Selection 7
    D. Training 7

Chapter 2
Operational Objectives and the Characteristics of Organizations That Implement Successful Projects 9

OPERATIONAL OBJECTIVES 10
    A. To reach the poorest sector of the economically active 10
    B. To aid more female business owners 10
    C. To have each project help a significant number of businesses 10
    D. To cover operational costs through interest charges and user fees 10
    E. To create or strengthen private organizations that assist micro-enterprises 11
    F. To support micro-enterprise organizations 11
RELATIONSHIP BETWEEN RESOURCE AND IMPLEMENTING ORGANIZATIONS 11
    A. Resource organization 12
    B. Local (implementing) organization 12
SELECTING IMPLEMENTING ORGANIZATIONS 13
    A. Flexibility and willingness to serve the poor efficiently 13
    B. Leadership 13
    C. Decentralized organizational structure 13
    D. Cooperation with beneficiaries 13
    E. Operational goals consistent with ACCION 14
    F. Avoidance of paternalism 14
    G. Ability to manage a loan fund 14

Chapter 3
Planning and Implementing the Project 15

LEARNING ABOUT THE COMMUNITY AND POTENTIAL BORROWERS 16
    A. Some specific questions 17
    B. Background research on potential borrowers 18
PLANNING THE PROJECT 22
    A. Types of projects 23
    B. Operational requirements 24

C. Financial requirements 30
D. Setting up a loan fund 32
OUTREACH 33

Chapter 4
Solidarity-Group Projects 36

A. Objectives 37
B. Eligibility for solidarity-group membership 37
C. Basis for forming a group 39
D. Group orientation 39
E. General credit policy 42
F. Other credit-policy considerations 44
G. Some specific policies for revolving-loan and savings funds in Colombia 46
H. Ongoing training of borrowers 47
I. Field-staff visits to groups 48
J. General meetings 48
K. Graduation 49

Chapter 5
Individual-Loan Projects 50

THE ADEMI PROJECT METHODOLOGY: SANTO DOMINGO, DOMINICAN REPUBLIC 52
A. First orientation meeting 52
B. Visit to the work site 52
C. Loan disbursement 53
D. Follow-up visits and meetings 53
E. Ongoing training and meetings 54
F. Credit regulations 54

Chapter 6
Creating Micro-Enterprise Associations 56

A. Objectives 57
B. Activities 57
C. Steps 57

Chapter 7
Project Management 59

ELEMENTS OF EFFECTIVE PROJECT MANAGEMENT 60

PROJECT EXPANSION 61
  A. Branch offices 61
  B. Umbrella organization 62
  C. Central office activities 63

Chapter 8
Program Monitoring and Evaluation 67
CASE HISTORIES 68
  A. Indicators of changes in the business 70
  B. Indicators of community impact 72
  C. Evaluating project impact 73
  D. Evaluation study 74

Chapter 9
Board Development and Public Relations 75
BOARD DEVELOPMENT 76
  A. Legal representation 76
  B. Setting general policies 76
  C. Financial supervision 76
  D. Supervision of management 76
  E. Raising funds and resources 76
  F. Institutional and government liaison 77
  G. Public relations and education 77
PUBLIC RELATIONS AND RESOURCE
DEVELOPMENT 77
  A. Objectives 78
  B. Responsibilities 79

Chapter 10
Financial Reporting and Monitoring 80
  A. Monthly statistical report 81
  B. Financial report 81
  C. Auditing 81

Appendix 1
Monthly Statistical Report 83

Appendix 2
Format for Program Financial Reports 86

Foreword

Very poor people who survive by finding niches for themselves in which they are economically productive and useful to other very poor people, create what are known as informal, parallel or micro-enterprise economies. Theirs is a very basic form of economic life—an old form, too. In early medieval Europe, when the official and formal economic life was a stagnant feudalism, it was the landless, the runaway serfs, the vagabonds—the poorest of the poor, congregating in rudimentary trading settlements—who created a parallel economy, and in so doing laid the very foundations of our modern economic life.

No doubt the great magnates and courtiers of the time typically despised, denigrated and failed to understand the potential of what these poorest of the poor were up to. In our own time, too, governments and traditional aid agencies have typically denigrated and failed to understand the potentialities of today's informal economies and the micro-enterprises that compose them.

Some fifteen years ago, a Peace Corps worker in Tanzania wrote a description of what he saw happening there. When he failed to interest anyone in publishing it or making use of its information, he sent it to me for my own interest. What he described was failure upon failure of ambitious economic programs. On the other hand, he did see some successes. These successes were small-scale, make-do efforts of poor families and individuals supplying transportation, accommodation, shoes, construction materials and services, baked goods, and the like. Their success was very limited, not for lack of diligence, intelligence, or a need for what they provided, but because, for one thing, they lacked any access to working or investment capital. Their success, their miracle, was simply that they managed to exist and function. In sum, here were self-sustaining, useful little enterprises, being starved and unappreciated, while appalling economic failures were being well-funded and internationally celebrated.

Over the years, as opportunities arose, I showed this description to people whose positions, I thought, might lead them into assisting small enterprises of the poor. Not one response was encouraging. Some said the micro-enterprises were obsolete, destined to disappear as soon as the elaborate schemes of the government and the aid agencies gathered momentum. Some said the enterprises were backward and pathetic, not fit for receiving credit, but only charity. One aid consultant said that, far from being assisted, the micro-enterprises should be suppressed as evaders of taxes and regulations, and as unfair competitors of respectable businesses. Another agreed with my African correspondent's assessment, but said, politely and sadly, that realistically nothing could be done.

Fortunately, at about the same time, the same phenomena were being observed in Latin America, by workers for ACCION International, which had been established in 1960 as a forerunner of the Peace Corps, to foster community development projects such as schools, roads, and water systems. As they did this work, people in ACCION encountered the struggling micro-enterprises of the poor, and came to the conclusion that assisting them might be the most effective long-term aid. In 1972 ACCION began developing the successful methods and principles described in this guide.

The guide's primary purpose, of course, is to make ACCION's experience available to other organizations. However, anyone interested in economic life and how people contend with it under very difficult circumstances will find revelations and surprises here, along with good reasons for hope in milieus conventionally deplored as all but hopeless. In my opinion, students in economics and political science classes and schools of business would profit by reading it. It may also occur to some thoughtful readers that the ACCION approach would even be useful in rich countries for obdurately impoverished regions and cities where the gulf between "haves" and "have-nots" yawns and grows. Indeed, as this is written, programs similar to those of ACCION are being started in a needy area of Arkansas.

Like the micro-enterprises it assists, ACCION deals in economic basics. It combats dependency, parisitism and bureaucracy. It builds on honesty, thrift, diligence, ingenuity and cooperation. It promotes self-generating, self-sustaining, self-developing and self-respecting economic effort.

Old habits of thought die hard. Traditional aid, well meaning though it may be, has been subtly but deeply infused with paternalism, economic imperialism, economic sexism and racism. But nothing succeeds like success, and the ACCION approach and attitudes may now even be starting to affect and change traditional aid assumptions. A handful of established banks are now advancing capital through a guarantee fund to ACCION micro-enterprise programs. The Calmeadow Foundation of Toronto, the co-publisher of this guide, is now a partner of ACCION in three different Latin American countries, and has recently started up its own credit program on a Native Indian reserve in Ontario.

I know of no better antidote to traditional attitudes that are economically and socially stultifying than the experience and premises of ACCION.

Jane Jacobs
Toronto, Canada

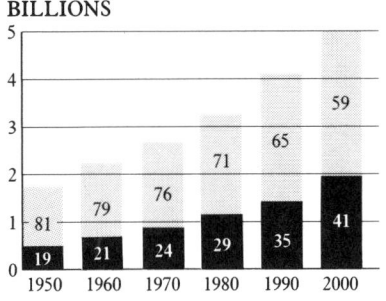

Third World Population
1950–2000

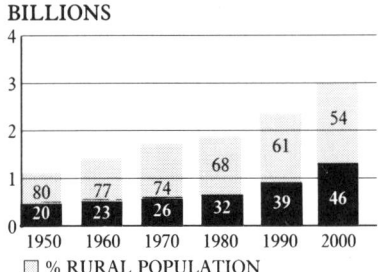

Third World Working Age Population
(AGE 15–64) 1950–2000

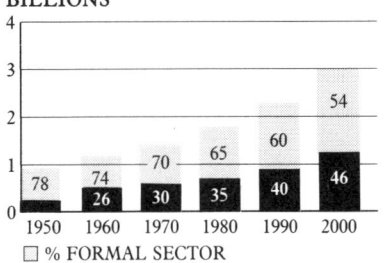

Third World Working Age Population
FORMAL/INFORMAL SECTORS COMPARED 1950–2000

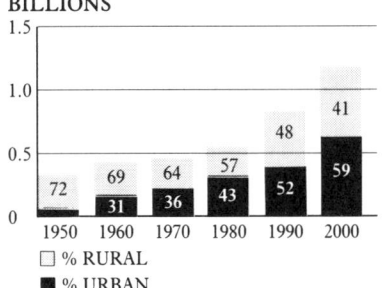

Third World Working Age Population
RURAL/URBAN COMPARISON (INFORMAL SECTOR) 1950–2000

INTRODUCTION

This guide was developed as an introduction to the planning and implementation of effective micro-enterprise assistance programs. It focuses on three types of assistance: credit, management training, and the formation of associations. Instead of providing a step-by-step recipe, the guide outlines an approach and a methodology that have been successful in diverse cultural and economic settings.

The methodology enables programs to reach a significant number of the poor at costs that are low enough for the programs to be financially self-sufficient. It distills the experience of numerous organizations throughout the Americas that are affiliated with ACCION International. Because their experience continues to grow, this guide is not a final document but rather an important step in continuing learning process.

The operational guide is designed for non-profit organizations, cooperatives, community associations, government agencies, and banks. While aimed at those who plan to implement micro-enterprise programs in the field, the guide may also be useful to private, bilateral, and multilateral donors and evaluators with an interest in the topic.

ACCION International and the Calmeadow Foundation collaborated in the design and writing of this text. We would like to thank the field staff of the various organizations who contributed to the content, and both PACT (Private Agencies Collaborating Together) and CIDA (Canadian International Development Agency) for their timely and generous support.

ACCION International
Calmeadow Foundation
March, 1988

CHAPTER 1
THE INFORMAL SECTOR AND HOW IT CAN BE ASSISTED

Recent research and project experience have shown that it is possible to assist even the smallest economic activities of the poor effectively and efficiently. Simple infusions of small amounts of credit ($10 to $500) over a period of one to twelve months, coupled with appropriate orientation and encouragement, can lead to significant increases in income, production, and employment. The best of these assistance programs combine quick access to credit with the best management techniques of the private sector, thereby enhancing the number of "micro-entrepreneurs" that can be reached efficiently and inexpensively.

THE "INFORMAL ECONOMIC SECTOR" IN DEVELOPING COUNTRIES

What economists call the "informal economic sector" consists of countless tiny enterprises begun by the poor in the cities, towns, and villages of the developing world. Hawkers shout their wares on street corners, mechanics patch vehicles in tumble-down shops, and "micro-entrepreneurs" weld iron grillwork, recycle used bedsprings into mattresses, make candy, or sew skirts and shorts in their homes or in small "factories" tucked away in back alleys and shantytowns.

These informal-sector activities employ from 30% to 70% of the labor force in the developing world. The percentages vary, depending on the country and the definition of what constitutes an informal-sector activity. In recent decades, the massive migration from rural to metropolitan areas has increased the number of informal urban enterprises in the Third World, both in absolute numbers and as a percentage of the labor force.

In Lagos, for example, 50% of all employment is in the informal sector. In Bombay, the figure is 55%. In Lima, it is estimated that 78% of the furniture and 90% of the clothing are produced in the informal sector, and that 85% of bus transportation is informal. In San Salvador, there is a business in 85% of the houses in the poorest barrios.

The informal sector is not only an urban phenomenon. In the rural areas, off-farm employment makes up 43% of the labor force in Colombia, 28% in Kenya, 37% in West Malaysia, and 33% in Iran. The fact that those engaged in informal activities are often the landless or those whose farms are too small to support them makes it especially important to assist this sector of the rural economy.

A. Characteristics of informal-sector businesses

Informal-sector businesses may be manufacturing, services, or commercial ventures. Despite the variation in size, type of activity, and degree of sophistication, these businesses share several characteristics:

- Small scale: People working in the informal sector often work alone or with unpaid family members.

- Labor intensity: With so few workers, there is little or no division of labor. Production is often manual, and equipment is simple and hand-made.

- Minimal capital inputs: Total investment in informal businesses ranges from a few dollars for the baskets and working capital of a street vendor to one thousand dollars or more for the simple equipment and working capital of a shoemaker who employs four or five workers.

- Local market: Informal-sector businesses are specifically oriented to the local market. They serve not only customers in poor barrios but also the middle and upper classes by providing many of the goods—clothing, shoes, food, etc.—that are sold in major stores downtown.

B. Importance of informal-sector businesses to the local economy

The fact that the informal sector is the largest and, in many countries, the fastest-growing part of the private sector makes it important to understand how these businesses function, what their needs are, and how they can be assisted. These enterprises are important for two main reasons:

- They will generate a majority of the 120,000 jobs per day that will be required in the developing world between now and the year 2000.

- They will provide a large percentage of the jobs needed for women, recent immigrants from rural areas, the uneducated, youth, and the very poor.

In addition, these businesses supply goods and services, teach skills, and provide entrepreneurial training (the typical shoemaker has a decade of experience as an apprentice and master craftsman before opening a tiny shop). Informal-sector businesses represent the most economical mix of capital, labor, and energy in a poor society. They also establish a vital link to large enterprises by furnishing the semi-finished component parts that are used by larger businesses to create finished goods for resale and export.

Tiny informal businesses are becoming increasingly important in most countries, despite obstacles to their growth, profitability, and very existence. They lack access to institutional credit from banks and other lending institutions, and as a result are dependent on moneylenders and suppliers who charge rates ranging from 10% per month to 20% per day. In addition, small informal businesses must deal with a hostile policy environment that considers most of these enterprises illegal.

ASSISTANCE PROGRAMS THAT WORK

Although some projects have failed, effective and efficient financial-aid programs *are* possible. Properly designed, they can bring about significant increases in income, employment, and mutual assistance. The successful programs have clearly defined objectives for both clients and staff, deliver services in a timely fashion, and are well used because their services reflect their clients' needs.

In general, staff of the better programs recognize that micro-business owners are capable individuals who have shown their initiative by starting an economic activity. Running such a business (no matter how small) requires skill, motivation, hard work, and an intimate knowledge of the local economy. Indeed, a staff's appreciation of the clients and the risks that these borrowers must take differentiates a successful program from an unsuccessful one.

The staff should gear their services to the owners of the smallest businesses, who may have little experience with banks and the collateral requirements for business loans. Reflecting these constraints and opportunities, successful programs must fulfill several requirements:

A. Work directly in the community

Project staff work through local organizations and forums to explain the program's services, identify loan candidates, and check references. Staff members go into the poor neighborhoods almost daily to visit borrowers and explain requirements to potential clients. Meetings are often held in the communities. If the project operates in a rural area, the staff will visit the towns and villages, perhaps once each week.

B. Simplify application procedures

In terms of payback, there seems to be little difference between projects that "write a book" on each applicant and those that reduce applications to two or three pages. It is more important to spend time with borrowers *after* they have received their loans, when their business's growth begins to strain their management capacity, than it is to fill out extensive application forms.

C. Extend credit quickly

Loan applicants become discouraged if they have to wait months before receiving services. They are accustomed to moneylenders who dispense money, albeit at exorbitant rates, on the spot. Well-managed projects extend the first credit within a month and often do so within one week. Subsequent loans are approved even more quickly.

D. Do not initially require books and complex business plans

An interest in better planning, management, and record-keeping tends to emerge as businesses grow. For this reason, training is offered after the loan, rather than before. Since only a small percentage of businesses at this level keep written records, only the simplest record system is appropriate. Staff should not insist that tiny businesses have the organization and working style of larger firms.

E. Do not require guarantees that would eliminate most potential candidates

Alternative mechanisms, such as "solidarity groups" and "circles," where three to eight micro-business owners are mutually responsible for the payback of loans, are an effective substitute for conventional guarantees.

F. Work with existing micro-businesses or help start others that are appropriate for the community

The start-up of larger enterprises is seldom successful because they require extensive capital inputs for extended periods.

G. Focus on the local market

Local entrepreneurs find "niches" where an outside expert may have thought none existed. Efforts to locate new markets for these micro-entrepreneurs are often more costly and difficult than expected.

H. Extend small short-term loans primarily for working capital

Larger loans for fixed assets are provided later, after the owner has proven his or her ability to repay the smaller loans. Small short-term loans not only "test" the borrower's commitment to repay, but also allow the borrower to see whether or not a loan will, in fact, help the business grow.

I. Charge interest rates at the market rate or higher

From the perspective of clients, quick credit is more important than a low interest rate. For very small businesses, the percentage charged on the loan is rarely a crucial factor in the business's profitability.

J. Allow loan recipients to assume a major role in promoting the program

Borrowers, with their network of friendships and their relationships within the community, form their own groups and provide one another with advice and assistance, which significantly reduces operational costs. At the same time, this intensified interaction strengthens their commitment to the project and to one another.

Perhaps the key ingredient behind the success of the ACCION approach is its emphasis on careful loan supervision and servicing. Field staff stay in close contact with the borrowers and their businesses so that if a loan starts to go wrong, they are quickly aware of the problem.

TRADITIONAL AND NON-TRADITIONAL APPROACHES TO MICRO-ENTERPRISE DEVELOPMENT

The characteristics listed above imply a non-traditional approach to small-enterprise development. This approach differs from the efforts made by traditional development organizations who provide extensive inputs to a few selected businesses. The non-traditional approach provides simple inputs to nearly all clients, in the expectation that most of the businesses will remain small while registering an increase in income. The few that do expand considerably receive larger loans and more sophisticated assistance.

A. Clients

Traditional projects tend to work with well-established businesses, attempt to create formal operations from informal ones or set up comparatively complex new ventures. Because of the nature and size of their clients' businesses, these projects must be highly selective. Many potential businesses may be identified, but only a few get assistance. By contrast, ACCION programs try to help all those who want to participate after the orientation process; the average size of the businesses assisted is much smaller.

B. Outreach

Since traditional assistance programs work with relatively few clients, they constantly seek new businesses to assist. Such scouting for new clients is a time-consuming activity for the project staff. By contrast, because ACCION projects reach so many businesses, usually concentrated within a single community, news of the program spreads spontaneously, and little staff time is required for promotion or client identification. A well-functioning program never lacks good candidates for assistance.

C. Selection

To grant the large loans needed to transform an existing enterprise or capitalize a new project, traditional programs require detailed feasibility studies, extensive training, and complete business plans. Due to the comparatively large investment, the risk is considerable for both the client and the program.

ACCION projects offer a more basic level of assistance in the form of small loans, primarily for working capital, and limited training. Because fewer risks are taken, the staff are able to delegate client selection to the business owners themselves. These micro-entrepreneurs then form solidarity groups among trusted and reliable peers in the community.

D. Training

In traditional programs, extensive training is provided before credit is extended. This minimizes the risk that a large, long-term loan will be poorly used.

In ACCION programs, initial training consists of a simple orientation and plan for using the loan. This is adequate since the first loan will only modestly expand the micro-entrepreneur's existing business. Further training and orientation is provided as businesses reach higher loan levels. Meetings with solidarity groups are held frequently so that micro-entrepreneurs can exchange ideas for improving their operations. These meetings work well because the businesses are simple, and useful knowledge is shared freely.

The success of ACCION's non-traditional approach challenges the following misconceptions:

- *"Credit alone is useless. It must be packaged with training, marketing, transportation facilities, technology, and education."*

The fact is that small business owners can use credit in small amounts to buy raw materials at a better price, increase productivity through improved equipment, and find niches in the local market to increase sales. Though other inputs may be important, they greatly increase the cost and complexity of the program. It is preferable to let businesses develop as much as possible with the simplest inputs—credit and encouragement—and consider other project components later.

- *"Credit to the poor is counter-productive. It imposes a burden of loans on the poor, who cannot repay them."*

Well-managed programs with loans tailored to the needs of the poor enjoy repayment rates of 98% or higher. Such returns reflect the profitability of these enterprises in even the poorest countries.

- *"The consumption needs of the poor are so pressing that any loans will be misappropriated for consumption."*

The participants' high repayment rate and evaluations of their businesses' performance show that most loans are used for productive purposes.

- *"The poor cannot save."*

Projects with obligatory and voluntary savings components indicate that the poor do indeed save. Moreover, the savings of borrowers can be an important factor in increasing the initial amount of the revolving-loan fund.

- *"Projects have little impact on income and employment."*

Projects consistently demonstrate that business income increases from 20% to 100% or more. One new job is created for every $500 to $1,500 of credit extended.

- *"Chronic poverty has a crippling effect on the mind and aspirations. The poor do not want to change."*

Participants recognize the capacity of these programs to improve their situation. Their enthusiasm shows an appreciation and awareness of the potential for change in their lives.

ACCION's experience has demonstrated that appropriate credit, encouragement, and the creation of supportive peer groups are the essential elements in the success of micro-enterprise assistance.

CHAPTER 2
OPERATIONAL OBJECTIVES AND THE CHARACTERISTICS OF ORGANIZATIONS THAT IMPLEMENT SUCCESSFUL PROJECTS

The techniques of the successful "non-traditional" projects outlined in Chapter 1 ensure that even the smallest businesses—street vendors, seamstresses, backyard mechanics—can be reached. It is important, however, that these techniques be supported by clearly stated objectives to guide the project designer and facilitate the project's monitoring and evaluation. Too many projects operate in a kind of "verbal fog." If staff members lack a clear vision of what they are to accomplish, it is difficult to make changes or determine whether a project has succeeded.

OPERATIONAL OBJECTIVES

A. To reach the poorest sector of the economically active

Loans and other assistance are given to the owner of any enterprise, no matter how small. These businesses include examples of petty commerce (collection of bottles and street-corner fruitstands); services (radio repair and hairdressing); and micro-industries of seamstresses, cobblers, and candymakers. Any activity that is not illegal and that enables a person or family to survive is eligible for financing.

B. To aid more female business owners

It is no coincidence that the smaller the business, the greater the chance that it is owned by a woman. Within its objective of reaching the poorest among the economically active, ACCION has tried to include more women in its projects.

C. To have each project help a significant number of businesses

The number of micro-businesses is enormous and represents an untapped market for institutional credit. In recent years, ACCION has developed several projects that have helped over one thousand businesses per year at one-fifth to one-tenth the cost per dollar of the "traditional" methodology.

D. To cover operational costs through interest charges and user fees

The concept that a service program for the poor can and should be self-supporting is innovative and even controversial, yet several of the ACCION-assisted programs cover their costs. ACCION achieves financial self-sufficiency when the interest charged on loans and other fees covers the costs of training and administering the loan fund. A strict definition of self-sufficiency includes the cost of capital (if it has not been donated), a reserve for losses, and the recapitalization of the loan fund to cover losses from inflation.

ACCION programs are projected to become financially self-sufficient in three years. Project self-sufficiency is crucial for three reasons. First, it frees the programs from reliance on donors. Second, it encourages the staff to graduate borrowers from the program into the formal sector. Finally, self-sufficiency attracts private capital from either commercial banks or other sources because cost-effective, relatively large-scale projects, such as the Grameen Bank, which reaches 250,000 landless poor in Bangladesh, are more easily financed.

E. To create or strengthen private organizations that assist micro-enterprises

ACCION supports local private organizations by training their staff to serve the needs of micro-enterprises on a long-term basis. As a resource organization, ACCION assists indigenous private organizations and builds local support for the informal sector.

F. To support micro-enterprise organizations

Micro-entrepreneurs in the informal sector are isolated. No one represents their interests before local and national authorities, and they lack a forum for sharing their experience and broadening contacts. ACCION has experimented with various ways of promoting micro-business organizations and has found that the borrowers themselves should decide which type of organization they prefer. The local institution merely counsels the micro-entrepreneurs in setting up and developing their own organization.

RELATIONSHIP BETWEEN RESOURCE AND IMPLEMENTING ORGANIZATIONS

The best micro-enterprise program often involves a partnership between an indigenous organization and an outside organization; the program draws on the relative strength of each. In providing resources, ACCION has worked with existing indigenous agencies and has helped create new ones.

The relationship between the resource and local organizations should be clarified in a signed agreement. Each organization has typical responsibilities:

Relationship and roles of resource and implementing organizations

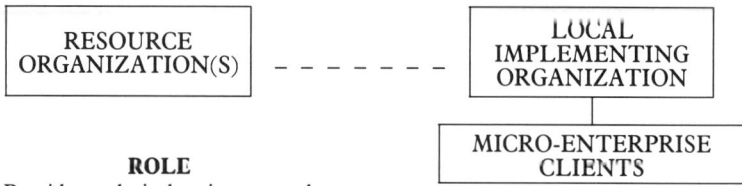

ROLE
1. Provides technical assistance and training to local implementing organization
2. Mobilizes financial resources for loan fund, implementing organization's operational costs, and its own costs
3. Serves as link between implementing organization and other programs
4. May carry out evaluation work of the program

ROLE
1. Directly implements the training, credit, and organizing components of program
2. Mobilizes local and international financial resources
3. Establishes links with local banks and other local entities

A. Resource organization

1. **Financial assistance:** The resource organization determines the amount of financial assistance that is available and the activities to which the funds should be directed (operational expenses, training, technical assistance, etc.).

2. **Funding:** The resource organization can procure or facilitate grants and contributions from large donors for the program.

3. **Technical assistance and training:** The resource organization can provide training through a full-time resident advisor, short visits of its staff, or by sending local personnel to other programs for training.

4. **Information and networking:** The resource organization can serve as a liaison and channel of information from other micro-enterprise programs.

B. Local (implementing) organization

1. **Administration of the program:** The local organization runs the day-to-day operation of the program, which includes maintaining an office and staff.

2. **Financial resources:** The local organization raises local funds to cover operational expenses and develop the loan fund.

SELECTING IMPLEMENTING ORGANIZATIONS

One of the most important factors in the development of a micro-enterprise program lies in the selection of the organization sponsoring it. The agency planning to start one of these projects should subject itself to a critical self-analysis. Can it provide direct outreach to the poor and administer loan portfolios efficiently? Can it distinguish between the dual objectives of social service and business management?

ACCION's experience shows that the success of a program depends on the degree to which the following traits characterize the organization:

A. Flexibility and willingness to serve the poor efficiently

Few government micro-enterprise programs are effective, because they suffer from problems endemic to government agencies: lack of imagination and flexibility, bureaucratic red tape, political rather than business objectives, and so forth. For this reason, most agencies carrying out micro-enterprise projects have been local non-profit organizations and development foundations. Banks that have conducted excellent projects create special units that use a simplified methodology to reach micro-businesses and avoid the documentation required for larger loans. They allow loan decisions to be made at the unit level rather than at the board level; and they train their personnel to be philosophically committed to the project.

B. Leadership

The board of directors or the executive director must show a high degree of leadership. They must have a clear vision of the organization's role and an ability to motivate and instill staff with a sense of mission.

C. Decentralized organizational structure

Centralized decision-making is detrimental to a micro-enterprise program, because those in direct contact with micro-businesses should have the flexibility to make day-to-day decisions. If staff fully participate in making decisions and defining the program, they will be more committed to the organization and to its projects.

D. Cooperation with beneficiaries

Whenever possible, the organization should include the views and suggestions of the program's beneficiaries in its decisions. Periodic evaluations of beneficiaries by loan-review committees or the board of directors can ensure a high degree of cooperation between the organization and its clients.

E. Operational goals consistent with ACCION
The organization should share the operational objectives that were described at the start of the chapter.

F. Avoidance of paternalism
Many agencies have a tradition of social service and are not accustomed to dealing with beneficiaries as business clients. A micro-enterprise program must deal with micro-entrepreneurs in a professional manner. The clients can manage their own businesses and are capable of development. The program's role is to help them achieve their goals, and the micro-entrepreneurs should be treated as clients with financial obligations. Since loans are a form of assistance that, by definition, are repaid, clients must be made aware of the consequences of neglecting their obligation.

G. Ability to manage a loan fund
Good management of a credit program requires that the organization be capable of dealing with certain financial concepts and exercising adequate control over the loan portfolio.

Chapter 3
Planning and Implementing the Project

LEARNING ABOUT THE COMMUNITY AND POTENTIAL BORROWERS

The first task is to carry out a feasibility study to learn as much as possible about potential micro-business clients. This study should take about two months. During this period vital knowlege will be acquired about the area, the business owners, the local institutions, and the leaders in the community who can help the project succeed. As the first month's objective, the agency should gain the community's backing for the project. If people see the new venture as an intrusion or allied with a particular faction, they will be less likely to accept it. The second month will focus on a more formal survey of the micro-enterprises that the project will ultimately serve.

The feasibility study is based on individual and group interviews with business owners (and prospective entrepreneurs) referred by other business owners or leaders in the community. Referrals will minimize suspicion and help identify likely candidates for future participation. The group interviews are particularly important since they set the tone for group meetings and for the active participation that is needed for the project to succeed.

Staff should make their initial visits to each area in the company of someone who knows the community and its leaders, and is known and respected by them. Ideally the person will be interested in the kind of grassroots development implicit in the project.

Throughout the study, the agency should be aware of the basic "climate" of each meeting by checking whether

- the attitude is one of hope or despair;

- the attitude is open, informative, and collaborative, or reserved and hostile;

- the community (or, lacking that, any individual) is taking or has ever taken any action to stimulate the economy.

The following information can be obtained from secondary sources and may assist the research:

- Population: number, increase, decrease
- Number of registered businesses: increase, decrease
- Number of businesses in different size categories
- Number of self-employed: increase, decrease
- Unemployment, under-employment
- Average income, population living below the poverty line

It is also essential to get a feel for the community through direct observation and questioning:

- What does the main street look like? Is there evidence of new construction, general cleanliness, and attractiveness? Does the community see itself as progressing? Is it proud of its accomplishments?

- What is it like in the good parts of the community? In the poorest sections? Note who lives there, the level of housing, the level of services, the quality of streets, drainage, water, and electricity. Look for evidence of small businesses or income-generating activity on the streets, inside houses, or in shops. What is the density of informal-sector activity? Note any signs that advertise community organizations, service clubs, or cooperatives.

- After the proper introductions, ask questions to get a sense of the local economy and whether or not individuals and organizations are behind the community's development. As the conversation progresses, information about the project can be given if it seems appropriate.

A. Some specific questions

Economic conditions

- Over the past couple of years, have more people moved in or moved out? (Follow-up questions: Why are people moving in or out? Where do those people who are moving in come from? Why are they coming here? What did they do before they came?)

- Is it easier or harder to find work than it was in the past? (Follow-up questions: Why is it now easier/harder to find work? How many people in the area are looking for work but can't find it?)

- Have more businesses opened than closed in the past few years? Which ones have closed? Opened? Why?

- What is manufactured? Who are the major employers? Which might become more important in a few years?

- Are land values and prices of houses rising or falling? (Determine the percentage increase or decrease.)

- Is there anything else bringing money into the town? (Examples: government installations, tourism, local hospitals, regional schools, etc.)

- (For rural areas) What is produced? (Follow-up questions: Are dairy cattle, beef, or hogs more important? What are the three main crops? Which one is most important?) Is there any mining ? Commercial fishing? Timber production? What is most important now? List all items mentioned in order of importance. (Follow-up questions: Are any of these more or less important than they were previously? Why? What is seen as becoming more important in the future? Why?)

- (For rural areas) Are there any local facilities (silos, grain dryers, dairies, sawmills, cotton gins, slaughterhouses) that need to be expanded or constructed to increase production or that would help encourage the production of new items? (This may help identify possible larger-scale projects.)

- In summary, what are considered the present bright spots in the local economy? What might become the highlights in a few years? Has anyone in the area recently started a business or produced something that could help the town's economy?

Community leadership
- Are there any organizations or individuals actively promoting the economic development of the community? If there are, get the names of people to contact, information on when and by whom the organization was formed, what it has accomplished, and what its plans are for the immediate and long-term future.

- List any other community organizations and get information on how active they are, what they have done recently, and what they hope to do in the future.

Banks, other financial institutions, and government programs
- How are local banks and bankers involved in the development of the town's economy? What are their policies for lending to the smallest businesses? What are their smallest business loans?

- Is the bank willing to finance micro-businesses? What would be required to get the banks interested? (It may be that local banks would be willing to put some of their resources into the fund if there were a strong guarantee for repayment of loans.)

- Are there any government programs promoting economic development? Describe.

- Is there a cooperative or alternative financing mechanism? Is it interested in small-business financing?

B. Background research on potential borrowers
After the first month of learning about the communities in the region and deciding which are best suited for the credit program, the second

month should be spent learning about the potential users of the loan fund.

The objectives of this stage are

• to learn to recognize the characteristics and needs of very small business owners;

• to learn of their plans for business development and determine how the loan project can assist them;

• to learn whether potential and existing business owners are receptive to using credit-guarantee groups in the projects.

The following survey is a typical example of the format used by ACCION. Normally a random sample of between two hundred and three hundred businesses is selected. Interviews are conducted by project staff or students hired and trained to collect the information. Once collected, the information is translated and analyzed.

Small Enterprise Survey

1. What kind of business do you have (manufacturing, commerce, service, mixed)? Describe. ....
   ....
2. When did you start this business? ....
3. Do you own this business (personally, in partnership, or by corporation)?
   ....
4. What do you make (if manufacturing)? Specify units per day/week/month.
   ....
5. What do you sell (if commerce)? Specify major projects and units per day/week/month sold. ....
   ....
6. What services do you provide (if service)? Specify major services and units, e.g., haircuts, per day/week/month. ....
   ....
7. How many months a year do you operate this business? ....
8. Who are your customers (individual customers/business/government/mail order/other)? Which is most important? ....
   ....
9. Where are your customers from (the neighborhood/this town/other)?
   ....
10. Are your sales going up? .... a lot/a little ....
                   going down? .... a lot/a little ....
              about the same? ....
    Why? ....

11. Are you working at full capacity/close to full capacity/about half capacity/ less than half capacity? ....
    If not at full capacity, why not? ....
12. Do you have another business? ,,,
13. Are you working for wages? ....
14. Who works here? ....
        you .... (hours per week) ....
      family or relatives .... (hours per week for each) ....
        non-family .... (hours per week for each) ....
15. What were your sales last month? Yesterday? In a good day? Bad day (establish four or five categories)? ....
    ....
16. Where do you do business (in your home/another location/a stall or booth)?
    ....
    ....
17. Where did you get the money to start the business? ....
    ....
18. How do you finance your business? ....
    ....
19. What are the main problems small businesses like yours face? ....
    ....
20. What problems does your business face? ....
    ....
21. If you could get credit and the other help you need, would you like to expand your business? Where would you like to see your business in two years? ....
    ....
22. Would you have trouble getting more customers? Explain. ....
    ....
    ....
23. How much would this expansion cost?
    working capital $ .... specify ....
    tools, equipment $ .... specify ....
    physical improvements $ .... specify ....
24. Would you need to hire more workers? How many full-time/part-time?
    ....
25. Is it easy/difficult/almost impossible for a business like yours to get financing from a bank? Why? ....
    ....
26. (Explain the credit guarantee group mechanism briefly.) Would you be willing to form or join a group like this? Why? ....
    ....

27. How could the business owners of this community help each other?
....

Observations:
Level of interest: high / average / low / none
Feasibility of plan: very feasible /
                        well thought through /
                        feasible / doubtful
                        very doubtful / impractical

Leadership potential: high / average / low / none
Comments: ....
....
....
....
....

Group interview

Try to assemble from five to ten micro-business owners for the group interview.

• Find out what kind of business each owner has; how long they have had this business; whether it is part-time, full-time, seasonal, or year-round; if they have employees; if they sell to local people or to customers outside the area.

• Ask if they think small businesses can find a market and expand in this community. What kind of businesses have the best potential? The least potential? Why?

• Find out if they feel they could expand their businesses. Ask each person what that expansion would involve and how much it would cost. Would any new employment opportunities be created?

• Ask about the availability of credit and other help for small businesses like theirs. Ask about other obstacles holding back business growth (lack of markets, bookkeeping, legal issues, lack of information, etc.).

• Briefly describe the group credit mechanism and get their reactions to it. If the reaction is negative, ask if they would be willing to join such a group if this were the only way to get credit.

• Explore how businesses in the community could help each other.

PLANNING THE PROJECT

The project's design should be based on the feasibility study. If the study is complete, it will indicate which services are most in demand among the potential borrowers, suggest the possible size and scope of the project, and point out other features to be incorporated into the program.

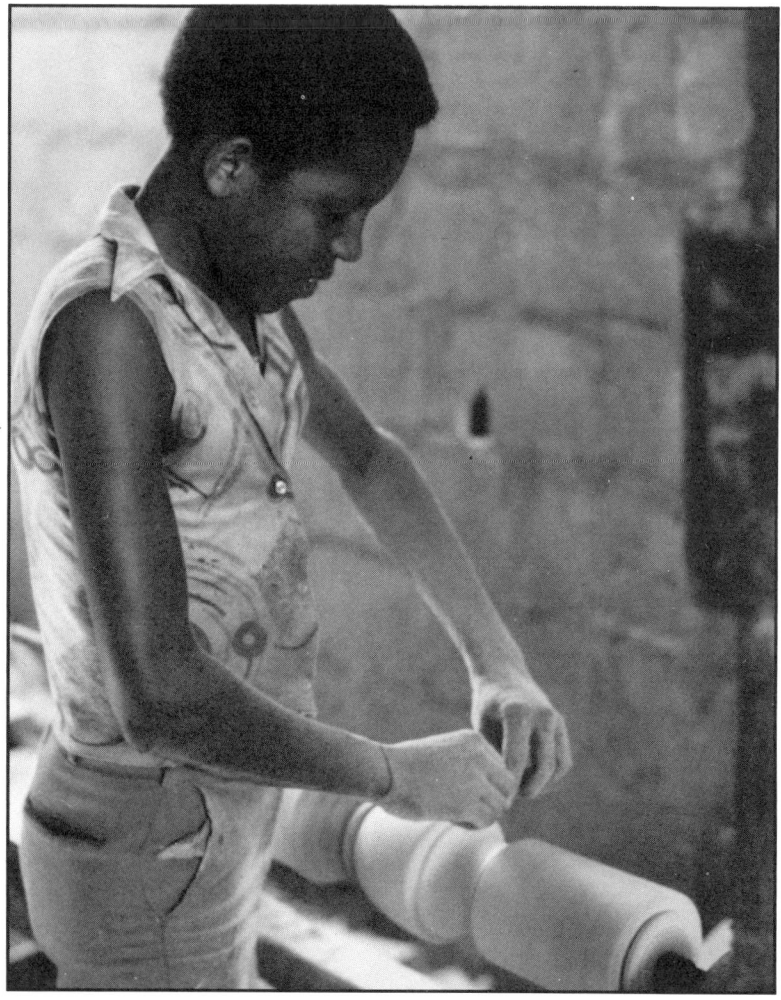

A. Types of projects

After defining the project's objectives, the first problem is deciding what size business to help. There are two types of ACCION-assisted projects: "solidarity-group" projects and "individual-loan" projects. The ACCION-assisted projects in Colombia and Paraguay give only solidarity-group loans; those in Mexico give only individual loans. Most projects offer both types, as in Ecuador, Honduras, Peru, Bolivia, the Dominican Republic, and Costa Rica.

Solidarity-group projects reach the poorest and smallest of the economically active: market-stall holders, street sellers, and the tiniest micro-industries and services (seamstresses with a single sewing machine, candymakers, hairdressers, etc.).

Solidarity-group members guarantee each other's loans, which eliminates the need for collateral, co-signers, and other guarantees. Loans tend to be small (from $25 to $200) and short term (from two weeks to three months).

Individual-loan projects tend to be more appropriate for owners of slightly larger businesses—those who can guarantee their loans with collateral and co-signers. These are usually the owners of micro-industries who have their own workshop and machinery, and two or more employees. Loans are larger (from $200 to $2,000) and of a longer term (up to six months or a year).

This does not mean that solidarity-group programs are not appropriate for the somewhat larger micro-producers who have their own shops and tools. However, solidarity-group projects are the methodology of choice for the smallest businesses. The solidarity group provides encouragement and security for those who have little experience with institutions, a loan guarantee for those too poor to have adequate collateral to secure a loan, and a far lower cost per borrower reached than individual-loan projects.

Advantages of solidarity-group projects
- *Peer-group guarantee mechanism*

  Because the members of the group provide the guarantee, the responsibility for payment, as well as the work involved in setting up the group, rests with the participants.

- *Low cost*

  Since the promotional effort and much of the orientation for new group members is assumed by "veterans" of the program, the cost of these activities is greatly reduced.

  Furthermore, if groups are composed of five or more members, only a single joint loan need be processed, approved, granted and monitored, as opposed to five or more loans.

- *Impact*

More businesses can be reached. In programs offering individual credit and management assistance, a promoter can typically reach 50 to 70 borrowers. In group programs, each promoter can reach 200 to 300 borrowers (through 40 to 60 or more groups). Accion Communitaria del Peru (ACP), for instance, is reaching 350 new borrowers every month, thanks to the group method. Each month it dispenses half a million dollars, a sum that would take individual-loan programs two years to disburse.

- *Self-sufficiency*

With low costs and high loan volume, solidarity-group programs can cover their operating expenses when, of course, commercial interest rates are applied on the loans. ACP in Peru, Banco Mundial de la Mujer, and Fundacion Familiar in Colombia—to name just three programs—are already covering their operating expenses.

Advantages of individual-loan programs
- *Individual attention*

The major advantage of individual projects is that the promoter can provide individualized business advice to each borrower. This is justified since the businesses are larger and their needs are more complex.

- *Larger amounts*

In general, individual-loan programs reach micro-industries that can absorb larger loans for not only working capital but also fixed assets.

- *More training and educational services*

Individual-loan projects provide more intensive training and educational services. Often the owner of a micro-industry needs managerial training more than credit.

B. Operational requirements

Once the agency has decided whether to use solidarity groups, individual loans, or a combination of both, it must decide how the project will be structured within the agency.

Operational requirements can be divided into three areas:

1. Organization

An organization that decides to add a micro-enterprise component must define how the project will fit into its organizational structure. Experience has shown that the project should be set up as a separate department with its own management and staff. These projects tend to expand rapidly and can easily overwhelm staff who have other obligations. More specialized staff can be hired over time, as the project reaches more businesses.

Figures 1, 2, and 3 show typical organizational charts: one for a new program; one for ADEMI in the Dominican Republic; and one for the Paraguayan Foundation of Development and Cooperation (Fundacion Paraguaya).

Programs usually start with a small staff and a simple structure aligned along general administrative categories. In the initial stages of the program, staff members may be responsible for more than one department. For example, the director might also be the operations manager. As the program expands, each of the departments will eventually require the attention of a full-time staff person. It may also become necessary to create sub-departments so that appropriate attention can be given to all administrative activities.

Figure 1: Typical organizational chart for new program

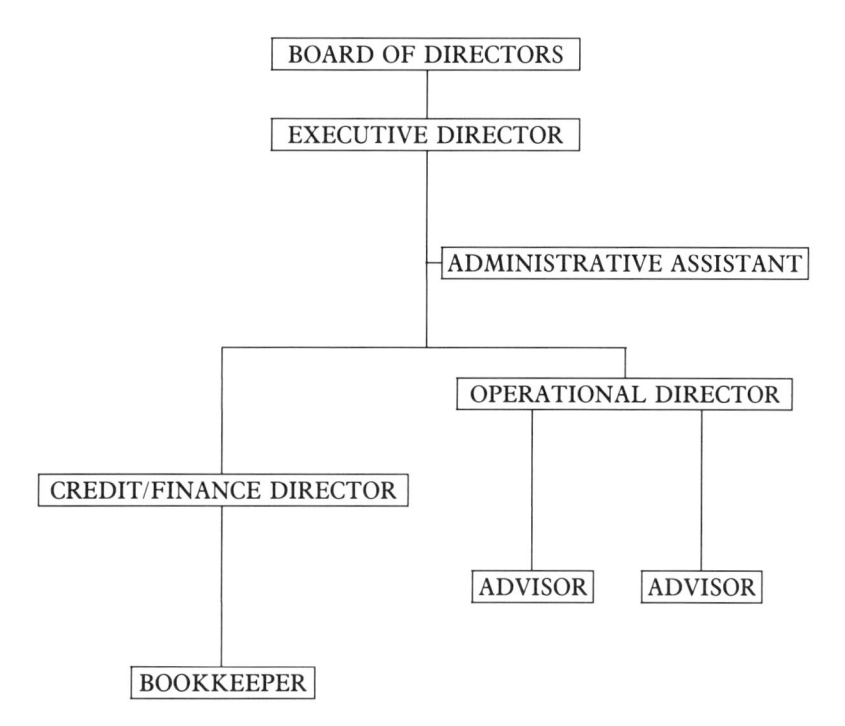

```
                    BOARD OF DIRECTORS
                            |
                    EXECUTIVE DIRECTOR
                            |
                            ├── ADMINISTRATIVE ASSISTANT
                            |
                    OPERATIONAL DIRECTOR
            |                   |            |
CREDIT/FINANCE DIRECTOR      ADVISOR      ADVISOR
            |
      BOOKKEEPER
```

CHAPTER 3

Figure 2: ADEMI (Dominican Republic) Organizational Structure

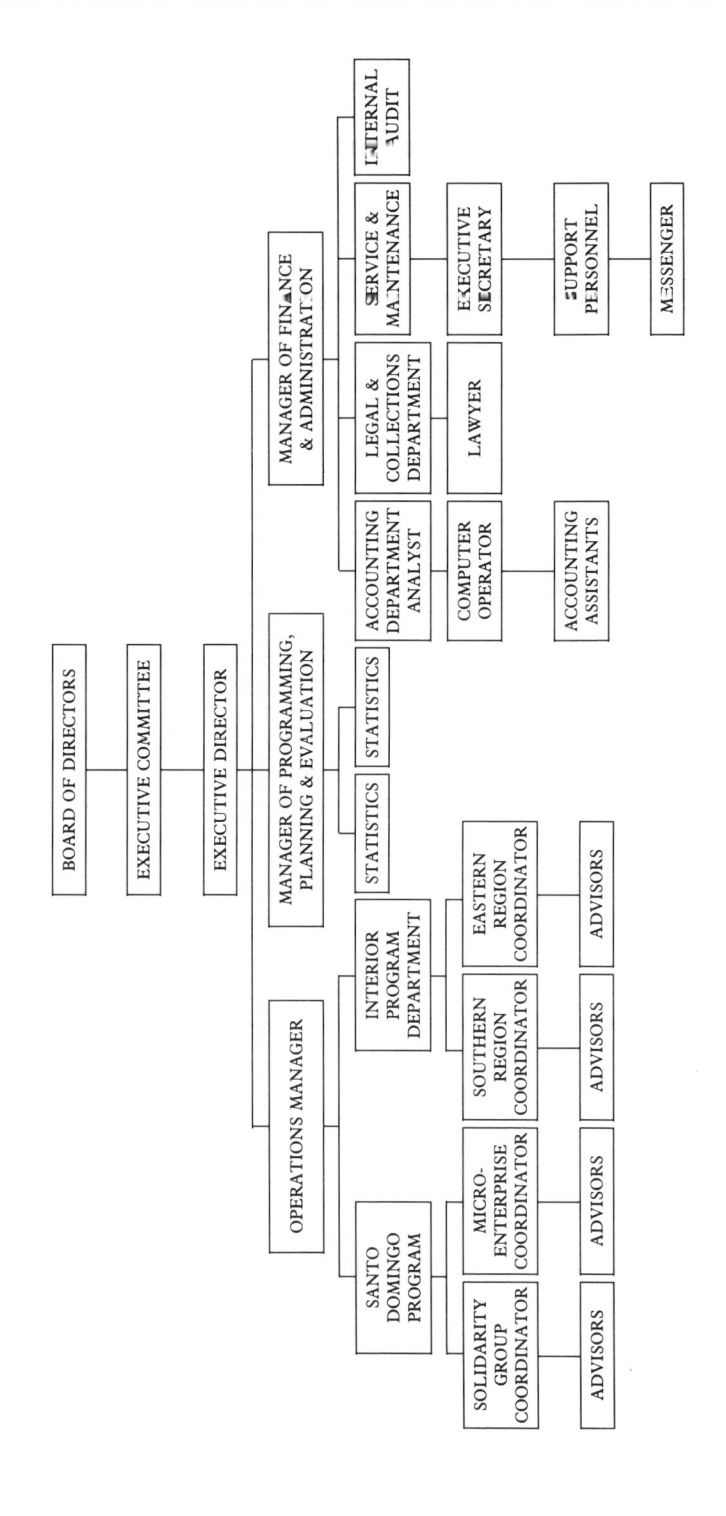

Figure 3: Organizational chart: Paraguayan Foundation of Development and Cooperation (Fundacion Paraguaya)

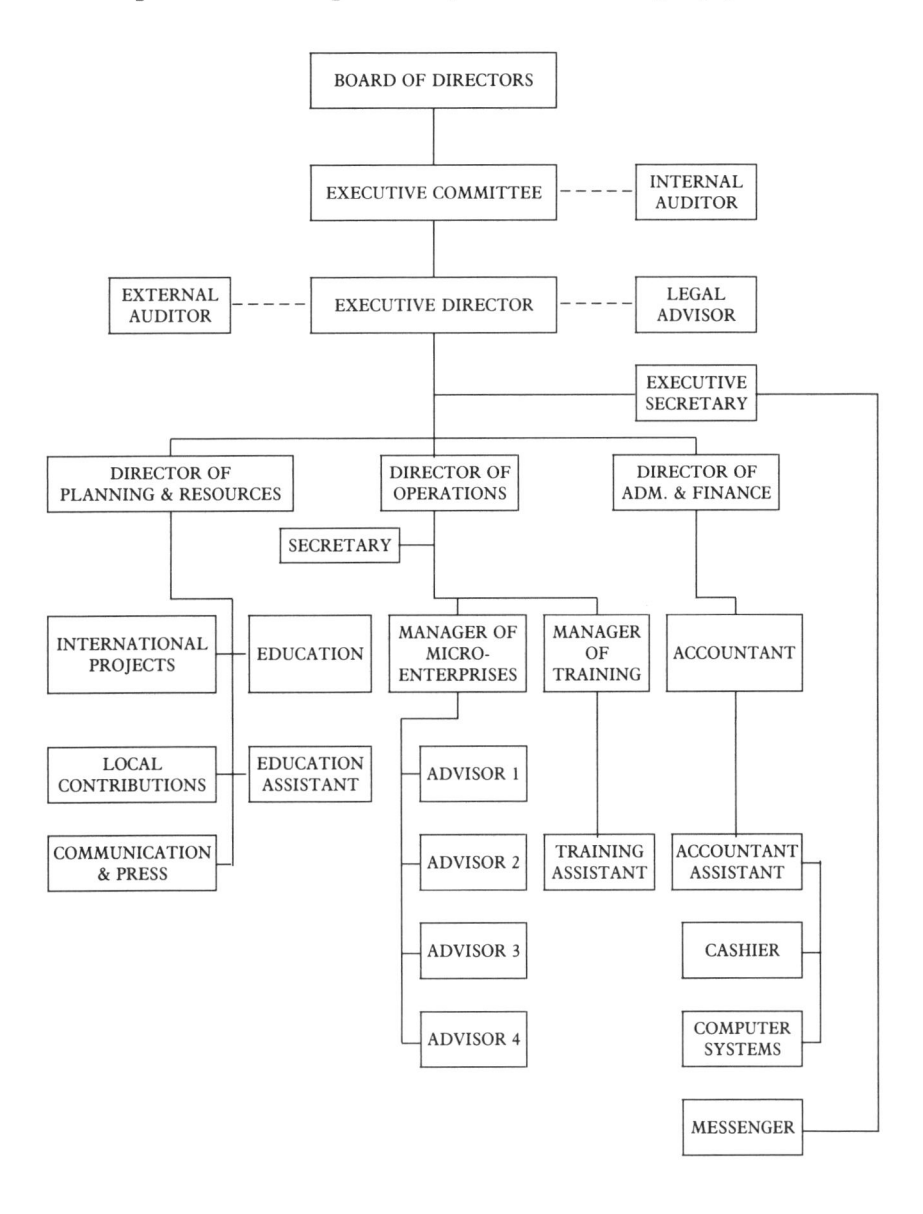

2. Staffing

Projects typically start with five to seven local staff members: the director, who may also serve as business adviser or promoter; a bookkeeper or accountant, who keeps track of the loans; two to four promoters; and a secretary or administrative assistant. In the case of a solidarity-group project in an urban area, by the end of the second year, a staff of seven should be able to extend credit and provide training for up to one thousand businesses organized into two hundred groups. Projects in rural areas will probably reach fewer groups because of the time spent traveling from the urban center.

As the project expands, more specialized personnel can be added in training, accounting, and supervision, but it is generally advisable not to add additional staff until there is a definite need.

a. *Staff selection*

The functions of the promoters and other staff of a micro-enterprise project go far beyond the traditional loan officers of commercial banks. In addition to discharging conventional banking responsibilities, the promoter must also serve as a social worker and agent of social change. Micro-enterprise staff must have the following skills:

- an understanding of the social and economic milieu within the region;

- an ability to identify potential clients;

- an ability to motivate groups and prepare them to receive project services;

- an ability to disburse loans as well as supervise loan recovery;

- an ability to render required technical services as demanded by the borrowers;

- a knowledge of office administration.

It is not easy to find people who can take on the role of project staff. Perhaps the most important requirement is attitude—staff that identify with the project's goals and are committed to working with the poor. If any staff members believe it is beneath their level of skill to work with micro-businesses, they might be condescending and arrogant in their dealings with project clients. Similarly, if they see these clients as dependent persons with little potential for improving themselves, they might be paternalistic in their approach.

Ideally, a staff person should be willing to work long hours, often outside the usual office schedule. The staff person should have a desire to provide a necessary service without being intrusive, an ability to communicate well with people at various social levels, and an appreciation for the micro-entrepreneurs and the activities in which they are engaged. Typically, the field staff will be young, educated, and socially conscious. Because of the many female clients, special care must be taken to hire individuals who are sensitive to the particular constraints encountered by women entrepreneurs.

b. *Job descriptions*

Executive Director: responsible to the Executive Committee and Board of Directors for the administration and operation of the program. Principal responsibilities include

- hiring and supervising program personnel;
- financial and operational administration of the program;
- establishing relationships with financial supporters (fundraising);
- program development;
- development of manuals and operational guidelines.

Operations Manager: responsible for the design and implementation of all program activities. Principal responsibilities include

- coordination of solidarity-group and micro-enterprise programs;
- development and implementation of training and technical assistance to clients;
- hiring, training, and supervising field staff;
- management of loan disbursement and collection.

Director of Finance and Administration: responsible for the financial and legal aspects of both the program and the organization.

Administrative Assistant or Secretary: responsible for the management of the office.

Field Promoter or Advisor: responsible for providing clients with technical assistance in business administration, bookkeeping, and financial management. The promoter is the chief liaison between the clients and the program. Principal responsibilities include

- promoting the program and identifying new clients;
- evaluating potential clients;
- assisting clients in the loan-application process;
- evaluating the program's impact.

3. Equipping the office

Each project needs basic office equipment to operate efficiently. This should include a desk and chair for each of the office staff, calculators for the field promoters, a small computer for the accountant, and a typewriter and file cabinets for the secretary. Other basic equipment includes tables and folding chairs for meetings and simple audio-visual equipment.

In all but the most densely populated areas, field staff must have their own transportation if they are to work efficiently. Small motorcycles are usually the best mode of transport.

C. Financial requirements

A project budget should have three components: operations (including staff, equipment, overhead, etc.), the loan fund, and technical assistance from a resource organization.

Accounting system

In most cases, accounting systems used by non-profit organizations are inadequate to manage a credit program. Before starting up operations, it is important to set up a computerized accounting system, preferably one that integrates loan-portfolio management with general accounting. Computers greatly ease the burden of bookkeeping. (Computer programs specifically designed for micro-enterprise programs are now available from ACCION, for use on IBM or Apple equipment.)

Financial projections

Accurate cash-flow projections are critical for effective administration of a credit program. The following factors should be considered when preparing a cash-flow projection:

1. Loan-fund activity
  - market potential or demand for credit services
  - a schedule of loan disbursement and amortization
  - terms and fees for services (interest, late payment, training sessions, etc.)
  - cost (interest rate) of loan funds

The schedule of loan-fund disbursements and receipts should be incorporated into a cash-flow statement with all income and expenses for the program. The purpose of the financial projection is to provide an overview of the program's *total* cash flow. However, in order to evaluate the program's capacity for self-sufficiency, it is a good idea to separate program-generated income from grants and loans.

CREDIT PROGRAM CASH-FLOW PROJECTION

Month
1 2 3 4 5 6 7 8 9

Beginning balance

Receipts

Contracts/services
Loan repayment
   —principal
   —interest
Other

Total receipts

Expenditures

Investments
Operational expenses
   —salaries
   —office expenses
   —equipment
   —travel
   —overhead
   —technical assistance
   —other
Repayment on lines of credit
   —principal
   —interest
Loans disbursed

Total expenditures

Total receipts—minus expenditures

Surplus/Deficit

Other income

Grants/donations
Lines of credit

Net cash flow

2. Receipts
   - contracts and fees for services
   - interest income
   - amortization of loans
3. Expenditures
   - operational expenses (all fixed and variable administrative costs)
   - interest paid on loan funds
   - loan disbursements
4. Other income
   - grants and contributions
   - lines of credit

Financial projections should be made for three to five years and adjusted at six-month intervals, based on actual performance.

Technical assistance
Most organizations will need external assistance, particularly in the project design and early implementation stage. This cost needs to be included in the overall budget.

D. Setting up a loan fund

The program will most often manage its loan fund through a local financial institution. There are two basic options to consider.

1. Revolving account
One option is for the program to place its loan fund in an account at a local institution. Loans are disbursed by issuing a cheque to the client, who then cashes the cheque at the bank. Similarly, loans are recovered by the client making periodic payments at the bank which are, in effect, deposits to the program's account.

There are two main advantages to this option. First, the program staff maintain complete control over all financial decisions. The bank plays no role in screening clients. Second, the program retains all interest earnings from loaning out of the fund. In this case the bank simply has an administrative function.

2. Loan guarantee fund
The second option is to place the loan funds in a local bank as a guarantee against the money that the *bank* loans to program clients. In this case, program clients are issued a voucher from the program which verifies approval of their loan application. The client then takes the voucher to the bank and the bank makes the actual loan. The client is then responsible for making all payments directly to the bank.

In this case, the bank will earn the interest on the money loaned to the program's clients. However, the program still may earn interest on its deposits in the bank. This option has the advantage of encouraging working relationships between micro-entrepreneurs and formal financial institutions.

There are, in fact, variations on these options. For example, local banks may be willing to extend a line of credit to the program if it is backed by a standby letter of credit from a third party. For instance, the ACP program in Peru has successfully negotiated and used a line of credit from a private bank in Lima. To guarantee the line of credit, ACCION opened a letter of credit through a U.S. bank in favor of the Peruvian bank. This approach offers the potential for leveraging more funds than the bank might otherwise be willing to provide on its own.

Savings

Many programs require or encourage clients to maintain a savings account. Clients may choose to save at a local institution of their choice, or they may keep their savings on deposit with the program. If the legal structure of the sponsoring organization permits the receipt of savings deposits, these deposits can be utilized to further capitalize the loan fund.

OUTREACH

Once the planning stage has been completed and sufficient funds have been secured, the program can begin.

The "feasibility study" will have prepared staff for the implementation phase, starting with outreach and the orientation of prospective credit-guarantee group members. Staff will have decided in which communities to focus the initial work, made good contacts with the leaders of these communities, and solicited their active support. By this stage, the staff will have learned about the needs and plans of the business owners whom the project hopes to assist. The staff will have identified a number of business owners who would be willing to participate in the project. They will have interviewed many of the potential clients to determine their interest in, and reservations about, the project's methodology.

Ideally, during the "feasibility study" local staff will have been recruited and will have learned much about the region and the micro-businesses. They will have collected information, established contacts, and developed a plan of action. If possible, the local staff will be recruited from the area so that they know the communities and the social context, and have a commitment to the area and to the people living there.

Promotion and orientation starts from this base. Conditions in communities vary; the actual outreach and orientation strategy will undoubtedly reflect what the staff feel most comfortable with. Nevertheless, the following outlines a sequence of possible steps:

• Contact the community leaders whom you interviewed in the feasibility stage and solicit their help in telling others about the project. They can do this through their own individual contacts or by organizing meetings where you can explain the program.

• Contact those business owners who are most likely to join the project. Encourage them to explain the project to others.

• If it seems appropriate, set up an *ad hoc* advisory committee of community leaders and the most interested business owners.

- Announce the project in local newspapers; print up a brochure that explains the program, distribute it as widely as possible, and talk about the project on local radio and TV. This will reinforce the commitment of those whom you approached previously. (It should be noted that mass-media advertising often generates requests for services from the owners of larger, better-established businesses who are not priority clients.)

If the project works as well as hoped (ACCION's experience in Latin America shows that this is usually the case), the outreach phase should be relatively short. Word should spread from satisfied borrowers to other potential clients. If word does not spread, it may mean that the services offered are simply not attractive from the borrowers' perspective. At least initially, borrowers may judge the project by the time and effort it takes to receive credit. If they show little interest, find out why and make the necessary adjustments instead of spending more effort on promotion.

CHAPTER 4
SOLIDARITY-GROUP
PROJECTS

Solidarity groups consist of five to eight micro-entrepreneurs engaged in similar businesses. These small-business owners join together to receive credit, training, and technical assistance. The vast majority of solidarity-group members are very poor. In Colombia, for example, most members of solidarity groups earn less than the "minimum consumer basket" of basic goods and services. Few earn an income equivalent to the minimum legal wage.

The typical group member is a woman between thirty and forty, supporting a family, who has been working at her trade for eleven years. She works full-time, an average of nearly eight hours per day, six days a week. Half of solidarity-group members are functionally illiterate. Their businesses can be divided into two general categories:

Micro-vendors: sidewalk vendors, market-stall holders, mobile collectors and sellers of bottles and cardboard, and small shopkeepers

Micro-producers: small cottage producers of prepared food, clothing, and artisan products

A. Objectives
Solidarity-group projects encourage business growth, mutual assistance, and individual self-improvement. Their objectives are as much social as economic.

1. Economic objectives
- sustain or increase the real income of the poorest of the economically active
- sustain or create employment
- encourage savings

2. Social objectives
- encourage the beneficiaries to organize into groups for purchasing, selling, and other communal efforts
- promote the organization and participation of group members to represent their individual interests more effectively
- encourage individual empowerment by helping members to manage their own businesses and participate in the activities of the project

B. Eligibility for solidarity-group membership
Before extending loans, you should review the guidelines on selecting reliable borrowers. To show results, the staff of newly started micro-enterprise projects tend to accept any and all who apply. This is the "honeymoon" phase. Inevitably, some loans will not be repaid. How

can these risks be minimized? There are good and bad risks to any type of client.

The first task is to establish the parameters for deciding who is qualified to receive a loan. These parameters should be chosen with care, to avoid excluding those whom the project is meant to assist. Criteria that are too broad—giving credit to businesses that range in size from single vendors to small-scale manufacturers with up to twenty employees—work against poor clients, because the more articulate, better-prepared owners of the larger businesses (who also have a legitimate need for credit) tend to monopolize the time of the staff.

Solidarity-group members of a typical ACCION project share the following characteristics:

- Members are over 18 years old.
- Members have been in business for at least six months, or have a skill that can be turned into a business.
- Members have less than $450 of working capital.
- Members derive their income principally from the business and have less than three permanent employees. (Most work alone or have only one person, often a family member, working with them.)

Once selected to be members of a solidarity group, clients are responsible for the following:

- attend the information and orientation meetings;
- repay loans;
- participate in training meetings after the loan is granted;
- belong to a savings program.

Selection is an ongoing process to be done by the groups, not the program. Those groups that do not pay back their loans are ineligible for new ones. If an individual does not pay, the group has two options. The group can fail to make the complete payment, which renders the entire group ineligible for any new loans. In this case the loan outstanding will be turned over to a collection agency. Or the group can make the payment and be eligible for the next loan. At this point, the group may choose to remove the unreliable member and add a new person to the group.

Access to this line of credit will be important for micro-business owners and small farmers because they will rarely have an alternative source of credit. Another incentive for repayment is that they will receive progressively larger loans if the success of their businesses warrants an increase.

With this type of credit model, the job of the field staff is not to select, but to document that the person has a business, that it is within the size parameters of the project, and that the owner understands the project and has a workable plan for the use of the loan.

C. Basis for forming a group

1. Prospective members form solidarity groups by selecting friends and co-workers whom they can rely on to repay a loan. Existing mutual respect and friendships are the usual basis for forming groups. No more than two group members should come from the same family.

2. Group members should be occupied in similar economic activities of either selling, manufacturing, or services.

3. Businesses should be approximately the same size.

4. A group should consist of at least three members. The ideal number is five. Groups of three or four are often too small to repay the loan of a defaulting member and are not sustainable if one or more members drop out. Groups larger than five tend to lack sufficient cohesion. The maximum number can be flexible, but it should be kept in mind that groups are intended to be "small."

5. To facilitate loan repayments, members of a group should work or live near one another.

6. The majority of the group's businesses should have fixed locations. This makes it easier to contact the group.

7. Groups may remove unreliable members at the end of each loan.

Even with adherence to these guidelines, problems have occurred: the person responsible for making the group's loan payment has pocketed the payment; unscrupulous "organizers" have formed groups for a fee; and group leaders have formed groups with the prior agreement that the entire loan will go to the leader. Proper orientation, ongoing training, and periodic staff visits to each business can usually prevent or resolve these kinds of problems.

D. Group orientation

Project staff must make sure that groups understand the project's requirements and procedures before loans are granted. In the earlier ACCION projects, inadequate orientation resulted in a major repayment problem because the loan-group members did not understand their obligations.

Orientation occurs over a period of three weeks through a series of three meetings, each of which lasts two to three hours. These meetings should involve no more than five groups. Only groups with all members present should be allowed to participate.

First meeting

1. Project staff present the following information to the newly formed groups:

- philosophy, objectives, and overview of the project
- requirements for individual participation
- criteria used to form solidarity groups

2. After the initial introduction, staff should interview each group with certain questions in mind.

- Determine the level of acquaintance or friendship among group members and their commitment to the concept of the "solidarity guarantee." Was the group formed on the basis of mutual friendship and trust, or was it formed "on the run," just to obtain a loan (with little intention of paying it back)?
- Ask each member: "If one person in the group, for any reason, fails to pay his or her share, will you help make up the payment?" The way each individual answers this question enables the other members to decide who should remain in the group and who should be asked to leave.

3. At this point the staff asks a series of detailed questions about the business of one of the members. This should motivate the other participants to apply the same questions to their own businesses.

- What product is sold or made?
- How is it sold (for cash or on credit)?
- Depending on the type of business, how much is sold per day/week/month?
- How much is invested in merchandise or raw materials per day/week/month?
- Where does the working capital come from (savings, family, friends, moneylenders, or suppliers)? What interest is charged? Under what conditions is the money lent?
- What is purchased for the business? Where is it bought and on what terms?
- After considering the sum of sales less investment, how much profit remains per day/week/month?

These kinds of questions create a climate for discussing group members' businesses and provide a forum within which they can receive advice and comments from the other group members. By answering these questions, members start to analyze their own businesses. Once they see how to categorize such items as costs, sales, and profits, they can refine their plans for future growth.

Second meeting

1. The second meeting starts with an explanation of "solidarity" and "mutual assistance." Through "solidarity," group members can improve their position and that of their businesses and their families. In joining the project, they "belong to a movement." The following questions help to focus the discussion:

- What does the word "solidarity" mean?
- Why is this called a "solidarity-group project"?
- How do group members show their solidarity?
- When is solidarity among group members necessary?
- What happens when there is a lack of solidarity within a group?
- Can a feeling of solidarity exist between the group and the project?
- How can an organization of groups show solidarity?

2. The theme of the second meeting centers on the importance of the family business's progress and savings:

- Is it possible to get ahead in the business? How?
- How important are savings to family security and to the business?
- Is it possible to save? How?

3. Another theme of the meeting defines the functioning of the project and the implications of taking out a solidarity loan. In particular, it details the rules of the revolving loan and savings funds.

Before the formal constitution of the groups in the third meeting, each group is encouraged to consider carefully the membership of each individual.

Third meeting

1. Before receiving its first loan, the group is formally constituted as a "solidarity group." To fulfill the requirements of this stage, each group must do the following:

- Fill in the group contract.
- Elect its first coordinator and set up a rotation sequence for this position. The group coordinator is responsible for making the group's loan payments. This position rotates among members to divide evenly the time-consuming process of making loan payments and minimize the possibility that the group leader might pocket the loan payment.
- Give their group a name and number. (Members select a name—

usually something like "The Winners," that expresses their commitment to getting ahead.)
- Open a group account.
- Set the amount of credit for each group member.
- Select the day of the week on which to receive the loan. (Loan disbursements and repayments are staggered to improve efficiency and to avoid long delays.)

2. The second part of this meeting introduces the training and emphasizes the importance of bookkeeping.

The expected result of these three meetings is a cohesive group that is well aware of the benefits and obligations inherent in the project. Ideally the group will have a positive attitude for working together and a real commitment to the project.

The group methodology encourages a collective feeling of solidarity and a cooperative spirit. The members' first identification is with the solidarity group, to its commitments and responsibilities. Further commitment develops during the training sessions, in which several groups analyze common problems. These sessions promote the ability to think and work collectively. At a later stage, the members of the solidarity group take part in general meetings with the other participants, or in meetings related to specific business activities.

The training process fosters a sense of belonging and shared ideology. It emphasizes individual progress, mutual assistance, and responsibility to the project. Participants begin to "discover" that they have many rights: the right to work, to be free of exploitation by moneylenders and middlemen, to receive adequate health care, to live in decent housing. They begin to suggest what they can do to resolve their problems collectively: a solidarity fund to help members in times of crisis, visits to members who are sick, the development of an organization that can present their case to local officials, etc.

The task, both for the program and for the participants, is to extend and deepen the group members' participation in program activities, thereby paving the way to group self-management.

E. General credit policy

The credit policy allows loans to be offered to large numbers of people at low cost and with a good rate of recovery. The reasons for this are as follows:

1. The solidarity-group mechanism creates pressure for repayment

Group members are collectively liable for the loans granted to individual members, so group pressure keeps loan repayment high. If a group member cannot, or will not, pay, the other members of the group must make the payment. None of the group are eligible for a new loan until the previous loan is canceled.

2. Group cohesion supports members who miss payments

The fact that making the weekly loan payments is a responsibility of members as a collective rather than as individuals strengthens the group. In Colombia, almost 90% of the solidarity groups have made loan payments for members who could not pay in a particular week.

3. Loans are extended in small amounts and with frequent payback periods

When a loan is repaid, the next loan becomes immediately available. Repayment is either weekly or monthly, because it is difficult for borrowers to save enough for quarterly or less-frequent payments. For people accustomed to one-day and one-week loans from moneylenders, a one-year loan stretches interminably, and payback tends to falter after the fourth month. A group can carry an unreliable member for a month or two, but making payments for an unreliable member for a year can tear a group apart.

These small-loan policies work for the poor owners of businesses for the following reasons:

• The loan is no larger than what the micro-entrepreneur can immediately invest in the business and easily repay. Initial loans may be as small as $25 and are repaid in a month. Larger loans are risky. If the money is not invested wisely, the business owner is left with an impoverishing debt.

• The watchwords for the administration of these funds are "agility" and "efficiency." The first loans are available promptly after completing the three-part orientation session. Subsequent loans are offered on the day that the previous loan is repaid. In this regard, much can be learned from the moneylenders, who provide very small, short-term loans almost immediately. For them, the individual's reputation is the guarantee of the loan. Loan repayment is easy, with the moneylenders visiting the borrowers in their shops and stalls. All of these elements are built into the solidarity-group methodology.

• Small installments make it easy to pay back the debt without using all the working capital to repay the loan.

At the same time, these policies are beneficial to the project because small, short-term loans reduce the risk of loss. Proven borrowers subsequently receive larger, longer-term loans, while unreliable borrowers are weeded out of the project. Loans turn over quickly so that more borrowers can be served, and borrowers are motivated to pay on time because they realize that receiving the next loan depends on paying the previous loan.

F. Other credit-policy considerations

1. Simultaneous loans for fixed assets and working capital
Longer-term loans for fixed assets (machinery or tools) can be made at the same time as the short-term, working-capital loans used for merchandise, raw materials, and other short-term needs. New working-capital loans are only available if payment is kept up to date on the fixed-asset loan. One line of credit strengthens performance on the other.

2. Planning the cash flow of the revolving fund
Many projects are unable to meet the increasing loan needs of their original borrowers when the loan fund becomes totally obligated to more recent borrowers. The original borrowers become frustrated because they cannot get the new money they need even if they remain on schedule with all their loan payments. New borrowers, on the other hand, are anxious because they must wait for months to get a loan. If the cash flow needs of the revolving fund are not planned correctly, the project will face serious problems in loan recovery.

If the project fails to live up to its promises (immediate renewal of credit upon payment of the preceding loan), clients will begin to lose confidence in the entire venture.

3. Setting interest rates
Setting interest rates and fees that reflect operational costs (staff salaries, transportation, overhead, etc.) and the cost of money is a relatively new concept for micro-lending projects. It was assumed that the poor could not make a profit if they had to pay commercial interest rates, and that therefore donors or government agencies had to cover the lending costs.

The case for charging a commercial interest rate is a strong one. Indeed, the projects assisted by ACCION are charging a commercial interest rate or higher. Charging the higher rate is justified on the following grounds:

• Any survey of the informal credit market shows that these micro-entrepreneurs are paying rates from 10% to 20% per month to 10% to 20% per day for credit from moneylenders. This rate is from five to twenty times the commercial interest rate. The fact that micro-businesses are able to pay these rates demonstrates their profitability. These people understand that "the most expensive loan is the loan you don't get." Even at higher-than-commercial rates, the demand for credit is so strong that projects are unable to fill the need.

• Charging less than the real costs of running the project places the operating institution in constant need of new grants or subsidies.

• Subsidized interest rates perpetuate paternalism, with the assumption that the poor cannot make it on their own.

• Subsidized rates give the impression that the institution is "soft" on loan repayment.

• By charging an interest rate that covers expenses, the project is seen as a serious lending operation, not just another assistance program for the poor.

• Since one of the objectives of the project is to "graduate" the micro-entrepreneur to commercial lines of credit when the borrower's credit-worthiness has been established, the project's higher-than-commercial interest rates and short-term loans provide an incentive for the "graduate" to go to a commercial bank.

• Higher-than-commercial interest rates and fees make it possible for the agency to cover operational costs within two to three years. The real cost of subsidized interest is to the micro-entrepreneurs who may lose their only source of credit if donor agencies can no longer provide an operational subsidy.

4. Encouraging savings

Some projects promote and even stipulate a savings requirement as a condition for extending credit. The following are some of the reasons for requiring savings:

• It develops the habit of saving: no business or enterprise, however small, can hope to grow without accumulating its own capital. Savings encourage the saver to think about expansion.

• Money on hand is frequently spent on superfluous purchases.

• For the poor, any family emergency—a sick child or a fire—can use up precious working capital and put the small business owner back in the hands of the loan shark.

• With sufficient savings, the micro-entrepreneurs no longer need to take out loans.

- Experience in projects that require savings has shown that participants not only *can* save, but also enjoy saving because savings impart self-confidence and personal pride.

G. Some specific policies for revolving-loan and savings funds in Colombia

Rules governing the revolving-loan fund

1. Loans are exclusively for investment in each member's business.

2. Loans are extended to the "solidarity group," which is responsible for repayment. If a member defaults on his or her share of the loan, the group will have to pay on that person's behalf.

3. Group members sign a document providing joint and several security, and they accept liability as co-signers.

4. Working-capital loans to micro-vendors reach maturity after a period of fifteen days to three months. For micro-manufacturers, terms run from fifteen days to six months.

5. Loans are repaid either in one lump sum or divided into installments according to the institutional credit policy.

6. Partial-installment payments are not acceptable. If a member defaults and the group coordinator brings in a sum that is short of the amount due, the sum is received for deposit on account against a provisional receipt until such time as the entire amount due is paid. This holds up renewal of credit to the group.

7. For both micro-vendors and micro-manufacturers, loans may be increased by U.S.$25 each time a loan is signed if the borrowers can show their ability to pay and have a demonstrable need.

8. Follow-up loans are based on the good credit rating earned by the group. It is assumed that punctual payment of a loan automatically qualifies the group for the next loan.

9. Renewal of loans to groups that fall behind on their obligations depends on a decision of the staff committee.

10. Additional interest is charged on late loan balances.

11. Interest on credit is charged at the rate of three percent per month, or at the commercial rate authorized by law.

12. Fees charged by the organization should be adequate to cover the administrative costs of the program.

13. Loan amounts to both micro-vendors and micro-manufacturers should be between U.S.$50 and $350.

Rules governing the savings fund

1. Each group member must save a minimum amount every month. A suggested amount is U.S.$2 per month for each member.

2. Savings are deposited with the installments of the loan repayments.

3. If a member has accumulated at least U.S.$10 in savings and suffers a verifiable domestic calamity, he or she can borrow up to twice the amount saved, but not in excess of U.S.$100.

4. Loans from savings must be repaid in three months.

5. Interest is charged at the rate of 1.5% per month.

6. Bank interest generated by the savings fund is credited to each participant every three months.

7. Savers receive their own passbooks.

H. Ongoing training of borrowers

Training builds a sense of responsibility, understanding, and commitment to the project. The emphasis is on participation, sharing experiences among peers, and solidarity.

Training has two basic components: strengthening the values of cooperation, solidarity, and mutual assistance; and improving business skills such as bookkeeping, planning, and marketing.

If possible, not more than five groups should be trained at a time. Meetings should be scheduled at a time convenient for borrowers, which means that most sessions will be held in the evenings. Use of simple visual aids is a real plus. To avoid repetition, the themes covered in the training should be presented in a logical order.

The system uses a question-and-answer approach to promote self-esteem and creativity, and to strengthen solidarity. Teaching techniques use the dynamics of small groups to solve problems. This approach brings the experience of the group and their practical know-how into the training process. The teaching of subjects like record-keeping emphasizes practical application.

Acción Comunitaria del Perú (ACP) has developed a modular course plan for micro-entrepreneurs that covers the operational functions of a business:
- Introduction to Business Management (4 hours)
- Accounting (4 hours)

- Costs (4 hours)
- Human Relations (4 hours)
- Sales Techniques (6 hours)
- Finance (6 hours)

Additional courses can be supplemented for those who express an interest.

I. Field-staff visits to groups
During field visits, staff advisors discuss the problems encountered by the group and by the individual businesses. Staff show how to apply the management techniques that the group has learned to specific problems.

J. General meetings
General meetings of all participants are held periodically to help people get acquainted, become friends, share experiences, and prepare for

future organization. These meetings give participants the chance to evaluate the project and suggest changes. They also offer an excellent opportunity to present certificates to those who have completed their training, which serves as positive reinforcement for other people attending courses. Some projects organize meetings of micro-enterpreneurs in specific fields of commerce (apparel, manufacturers, shoemakers, retailers, etc.). This gives added support to businesses in the same field and further promotes organizational efforts (leagues, associations, etc.)

K. Graduation

There is no single policy for graduating participants from the program. Each project develops its own criteria. Below are some typical reasons for a graduating a client from the program:

● The borrower's credit needs surpass the maximum amounts loaned by the program.

● The business-entrepreneurial training program has been completed.

● The borrower has been with the program for at least two years.

● Financial independence has been achieved through direct business earnings or the savings program.

● Other financial institutions are available to make larger loans.

Although graduation is a goal of these projects, the implications of leaving the program need to be considered. If other institutions or banks are interested in serving the graduates, the graduation policy makes sense. If the graduating participants face a situation where there is no one to attend to their growing needs, they are better off staying in the project.

Chapter 5
Individual-Loan
Projects

INDIVIDUAL-LOAN PROJECTS

Although micro-entrepreneurs may be living in cities as diverse as Santo Domingo, Bogota, San Jose, or Guayaquil, their individual loan requirements have much in common. The following statistics describe Dominican business owners, but could just as easily refer to micro-entrepreneurs in any country:

- About 30% are under 30 years of age, but 48% are between 31 and 50.

- Though most have migrated to the city, 80% have lived in the same neighborhood for more than five years.

- In 70% of the cases, the business is the sole source of family income.

- Most rent their homes, but have a standard of living (demonstrated by the number of electrical appliances they own) that is higher than that of the solidarity-group members.

- Unlike the vendor or collector, the micro-entrepreneur owns a shop at a fixed location and has more invested in the business. More than half are tailors, shoemakers, and mechanics.

- Most work at one job; 80% started their own businesses.

- Their businesses were started from savings and the reinvestment of earnings, not loans.

- About 67% rent their premises.

- Almost 70% have business expenses under U.S. $500 per month, including wages, materials, and services.

- More than 80% sell their products or services directly to individuals. Although 83% think they can sell all they produce, almost half find it difficult to do so due to a generally critical economic situation, a shortage of working capital, and a lack of machinery and equipment.

- More than 80% employ three workers or less, and only 6% have six or more employees. In the city of Santo Domingo, the average business employs 2.6 workers.

- Workers have no specific training, and the demand for additional employees is seasonal. In general, 40% earn under U.S.$100 per month and do not receive social benefits.

- Only 5% use methods of bookkeeping, and only 11% keep any record of income and expenses.

- None receive any outside management assistance.

The principal obstacle to micro-business expansion is lack of credit, which is simply not available to businesses this small. Over 60% of micro-entrepreneurs feel that additional funds of less than U.S. $2,000 would significantly expand their activities.

An ACCION-affiliated project in the Dominican Republic extends credit to individual borrowers. However, projects in Honduras, Ecuador, and Peru are phasing out individual loans to reflect the new emphasis on solidarity groups.

The approach used in the Dominican Republic is similar to the solidarity-group approach in that it emphasizes small, short-term loans, minimal up-front selection, and technical assistance. Not surprisingly, the costs per dollar of loan are low.

THE ADEMI PROJECT METHODOLOGY: SANTO DOMINGO, DOMINICAN REPUBLIC

Below is a description of the methodology used by the Asociación para el Desarrolo de Microempresas (ADEMI) in Santo Domingo:

A. First orientation meeting

At an initial orientation meeting of micro-entrepreneurs interested in receiving loans, the following occurs:

- The ADEMI project is presented and brochures are handed out.

- The importance of the micro-business sector is discussed.

- The needs of micro-businesses are discussed.

- The credit system is explained. Short-term loans are provided initially, but as the business owners' ability to repay small loans improves, the amount of the loan increases. Loans are provided at commercial interest rates and are guaranteed through property, co-signers, and other guarantees.

- If the micro-entrepreneur still wants to receive a loan, a date is set for the promoter to visit the work site.

B. Visit to the work site

To learn about the business, the promoter visits the owner. During this visit, the promoter and the business owner write the loan application and decide how the loan is to be guaranteed.

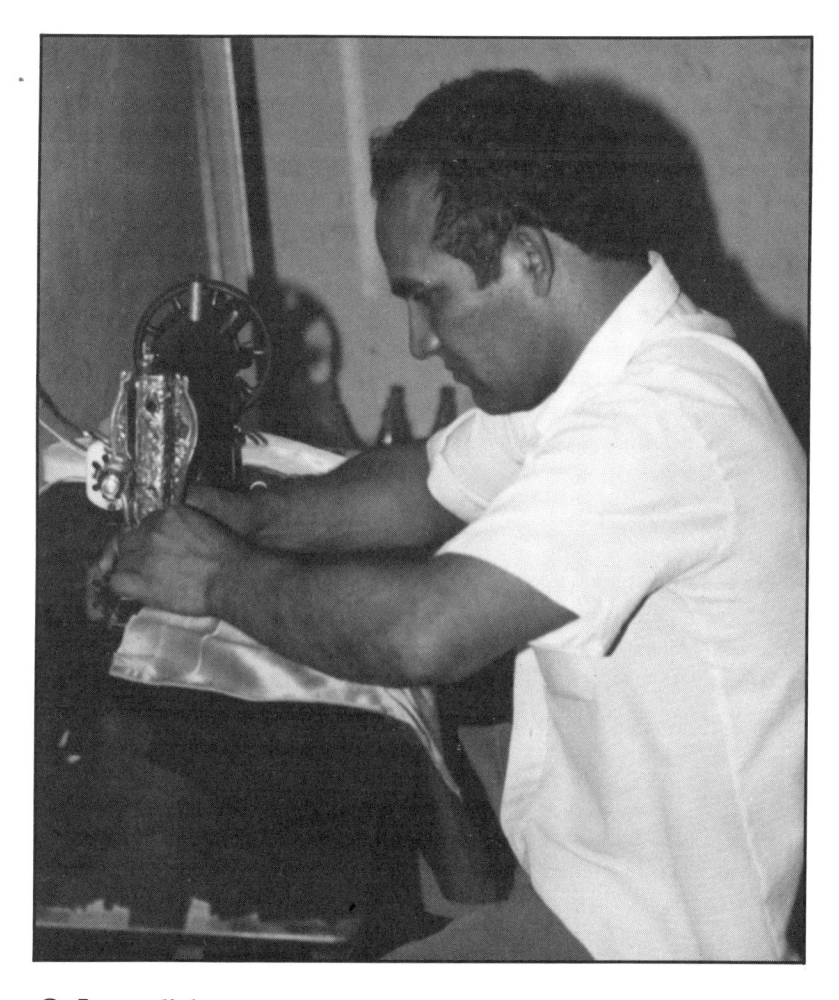

C. Loan disbursement

The credit application is submitted with the promoter's recommendations and remarks. It is approved by a credit committee consisting of the credit analyst and the executive director.

Once the loan is approved, the micro-entrepreneur comes to the office to sign documents and promissory notes. The check is then delivered. The borrower receives an ADEMI membership card with the initial loan.

D. Follow-up visits and meetings

A day before the installment is due, the promoter visits the business to leave the "Notice of Maturity" on the payment due. Applications are filled in for subsequent loans, and the business owner is invited to attend courses or meetings. There is a continuing review of the loan's form of investment, the business's progress, and the owner's plans for the future growth of the business.

E. Ongoing training and meetings

Short courses on business topics are periodically provided to business owners. Meetings are held to allow the owners of different types of businesses—tailors, mechanics, furniture makers—to discuss common problems. Business owners pay a cost-recovery fee to attend these courses.

F. Credit regulations

1. ADEMI will only consider informal-sector micro-entrepreneurs for the management-assistance or credit programs. Because of the small scale of their enterprises, these people find it impossible to obtain credit from commercial sources at reasonable rates of interest.

2. All candidates for ADEMI individual loans must be owners of a business that makes a product or provides a service. The business must be managed by one or two people who are responsible for all the important decisions. It must also demonstrate that it has the potential for growth if given a small amount of capital and technical assistance.

3. Micro-entrepreneurs should be willing to accept the requisite supervision and administrative assistance that ADEMI provides to all program beneficiaries.

4. Loans, without exception, must be used as working capital or to purchase equipment and machinery. The beneficiary must faithfully adhere to the use of the loan as stipulated in the loan application and contract.

5. ADEMI may, at its discretion, require as a security pledge the entire production of the financed activity, and equipment or other goods.

6. The principal security for each loan is the good word of the borrower. Each loan is to be represented by a promissory note payable to ADEMI and specifying the amount due and maturity date. Loans are to be granted to each borrower according to a gradually increasing schedule of principal amounts and terms. In this way, the program systematically initiates the borrower into developing his or her capacity to manage a loan effectively.

7. No new loans will be granted to borrowers who have loans in default.

8. Terms of payment on each loan will be established in accordance with the borrower's category and the credit schedule determined by ADEMI.

9. Interest rates on working capital loans will range from 2% to 3% per month.

10. In case of default, the borrower shall be liable for additional default charges according to the late-payment fee schedule.

Example

Time	Default charges
1-7 days	$2 per day plus 3% per month
8-15 days	$5 per day plus 3% per month
More than 15 days	Legal action

Note: A borrower who is taken to court for default on an ADEMI loan automatically loses his or her credit standing and may never again participate in the credit program.

11. Working capital loans to micro-entrepreneurs shall not exceed $5,000. Participants may only borrow at the maximum amount after working their way through the gradually increasing, short-term loan schedule and completing ADEMI's self-training program on the use of credit. After reaching a level of $400 in the loan schedule, ADEMI requires borrowers to attend management courses.

12. Fixed-asset loans shall be subject to different interest rates, and terms of repayment will be determined according to the borrower's projection of expected earnings.

CHAPTER 6
CREATING
MICRO-ENTERPRISE ASSOCIATIONS

In the countries where ACCION operates, the informal sector is characterized by a lack of organizations for micro-entrepreneurs. Micro-entrepreneurs generally do not join organizations, formal-sector groups like the Chamber of Commerce, or associations meant to represent their interests. One of ACCION's goals is to organize its program borrowers. All projects, whether they serve solidarity groups or individuals, promote the creation of an organization to represent micro-entrepreneurs. The form and structure of the organization—whether cooperative or a trade organization—matters less than the fact that it exists. Most important, the micro-entrepreneurs themselves must design the organization to serve their needs.

A. Objectives
The organization of micro-entrepreneurs should have the following aims:

1. promote the sharing of ideas, experiences, and contacts among micro-entrepreneurs;

2. allow micro-entrepreneurs to define their common needs and approach the authorities with a collective position of well-defined policies;

3. create new economic opportunities for micro-entrepreneurs;

4. supply social services to micro-entrepreneurs.

B. Activities
The activities that are appropriate to an association or organization of micro-entrepreneurs can vary. However, experience has shown that, at least in the beginning, activities should concentrate on the following:

1. organizing product fairs and establishing "showrooms" or other mechanisms to promote sales;

2. setting up a central wholesale supply and purchasing center for materials used by the businesses;

3. publishing a membership directory and offering reciprocal discounts to members;

4. offering a life and/or health insurance plan and setting up an emergency fund available to participants in case of disaster or illness.

C. Steps
The reasons for starting an association or organization of micro-entrepreneurs may differ. Nevertheless, the following steps usually lead to the establishment of such groups:

1. identifying a key group of micro-business owners who are interested in promoting the idea and willing to assume leadership of the organization;

2. forming a group of these individuals to discuss and plan the next step;

3. holding general meetings of all interested participants to present the idea, discuss aims, and share opinions;

4. electing an ad-hoc committee to work on setting up the organization;

5. planning additional meetings to discuss progress;

6. drafting and approving by-laws and other legal documents;

7. chartering the organization and electing a board;

8. defining specific activities to be carried out;

9. defining a strategy to finance the activities of the organization and recruitment of members;

10. creating the organization that will carry out the loan program.

CHAPTER 7
PROJECT MANAGEMENT

ELEMENTS OF EFFECTIVE PROJECT MANAGEMENT

Projects assisting micro-enterprises tend to fail not because there is inadequate demand or the project methodology is flawed, but because of poor management. The effective management of a micro-enterprise project includes seven major elements:

1. Well-focused goals and objectives

Too many programs have floundered because they did not clearly define what they were trying to accomplish. Even a project working exclusively in enterprise development can lose its focus. A common error occurs when a program tries to satisfy *all* the needs of its clients, adding more and more services until it becomes an expensive, top-heavy operation reaching relatively few clients. Successful programs concentrate their services in the areas of greatest need—access to credit and managerial training.

2. Project staff's commitment to the project goals

The staff members need to internalize the goals of the project. As long as the staff share a common vision and cooperate, the unit will tend to function smoothly.

3. Streamlined administrative procedures

Decisions should be made rapidly and moved through channels with as little delay as possible.

4. Internal controls

Good internal controls flow from clearly defined objectives and a flexible, efficient administrative structure. Records of loan applications, loan payback, and other statistics must be tallied daily so that the responsible field staff know immediately if a loan payment has not come in.

It is also important to keep track of the number of clients and payback rates in the portfolio of each field-staff person, so that one promoter's performance can be compared to that of another, according to agreed-upon criteria.

5. Incentives for local field staff

A well-run project should encourage local staff to be efficient. If data is kept on each staff member in terms of numbers of clients, payback, and other criteria, then the most efficient staff members can be rewarded. Those who fall behind can be encouraged to do better, and those who are simply not productive can be dismissed.

When the staff members feel that there are agreed-upon criteria for judging their performance and that the management structure of the unit enables them to do their jobs, they tend to do well. In this type of project, the degree to which the staff members identify with the work they are doing is quite remarkable. For an educated local resident, the work is simply more interesting and gratifying than other job opportunities.

6. *Inclusion of field staff in the decision-making process*
It is the field staff—those who spend most of every day talking to clients, providing management assistance, and dealing with payback problems—who best know how the unit is functioning. Yet a major complaint of the field staff is that their ideas are rarely taken into consideration because decisions are made at the top. Being involved in decision-making improves staff morale and provides a valuable source of information for improving the project.

7. *Adapting the methodology to client needs*
The learning process should be encouraged, and the staff should meet frequently. In one project in Ecuador, the staff met every week to review progress and make suggestions about how procedures could be improved. This resulted in a rapidly improved project methodology and strong staff identification with the project.

PROJECT EXPANSION

After the project has operated successfully for one to three years, a decision might be made to open more offices or incorporate other local organizations to cover a city, region, or entire country. Simply expanding the central office to serve several thousand borrowers is not recommended. Large offices quickly become bureaucratic, impersonal, and intimidating to borrowers. The close contact with individual clients, and the client's rapport with the staff, which is so important to successful projects, is soon lost. Rural areas need smaller branch offices because it can take potential clients and borrowers too long to get to a central office.

ACCION has experimented with two approaches to project expansion: either the implementing agency forms more branch offices, or an "umbrella organization" is set up to encourage new organizations to assist micro-enterprises.

A. Branch offices
The principal feature of this model is that the operating institution increases the number of borrowers by opening branches or sub-offices, either in the same city or in other towns and regions. The central office

then manages the branches. There are both advantages and drawbacks to this model:

Advantages
- Works well in a culturally homogeneous small country, region, or large city.
- Offers better control over methodology, finances, and services.
- Benefits from the economies of scale (e.g., in the use of computers).
- Gathers resources from donor agencies more efficiently.
- Allows quicker implementation of projects and programs.
- Cuts operational costs.

Drawbacks
- If the model fails, the program fails.
- The program can tend to become bureaucratic.

B. Umbrella organization

In this model, new organizations are encouraged to assist the same type of micro-enterprise projects.

Advantages
- Suitable for large countries or culturally heterogeneous regions.
- Promotes greater creativity in the project design and in the services offered by the projects. Each project develops its own variation of the methodology.
- May provide access to different donor agencies.
- May promote closer identification with borrowers at the local level and offer greater negotiating power or capacity for political pressure at the local level.
- Projects can be more stable (if one institution fails, the rest of the program can still survive).
- Allows a greater number of local institutions to develop their administrative capacity.

Drawbacks
- Costs tend to be higher and some functions are duplicated.
- Different methodologies make it difficult to integrate the services provided by the umbrella organization.

- There is less control over program objectives and methodology.

C. Central office activities

Whatever the model, a central office or department should be set up to direct the expansion. If only two or three branch offices are to be set up, the project's executive director can manage the expansion. In the case of the "umbrella" model, a separate unit (with perhaps one or two staff members) will encourage organizations to start micro-enterprise projects.

Maintaining a balance between centralized decision-making and delegating decisions to the branches or projects is vital for the long-term success of the expansion efforts. The clients of the central office are the branches or projects—not the individual loan recipients. While the central office sets the parameters for eligible borrowers and the categories of loan sizes, the local staff members decide who will be granted a loan.

This is important for several reasons. The most obvious are the reduction of paper work in the central office and the speeding up of the loan-approval process. More subtly, micro-enterprise programs work well when they have a personal relationship with their clients and a mechanism for selection based on the community's knowledge of who is or is not reliable. The central office cannot make these decisions efficiently.

Decentralizing much of the decision-making to the branches or projects has other advantages. It develops the local staff's rapport with the local clients, assigns them responsibility for the success or failure of the branch office or project, improves their decision-making ability, and makes the work more challenging.

The work of the central office should be carried out largely by the central office's field staff. Each field representative should be responsible for five to ten branches or projects, depending on the amount of supervision necessary. Field representatives carry out activities as varied as training local staff, discussing management difficulties with the directors, identifying problems, accompanying the local staff on their visits to clients, and participating in training activities with clients. The central office could be funded through a monthly levy charged to each project or branch.

The importance of a well-functioning central office is underscored by the experiences of projects that have expanded faster than their central offices could adequately handle. The rapid expansion left many units either failing or barely functioning. The rehabilitation of failed or failing units is a very slow administrative process.

Although the central office or expansion department does not grant loans or collect savings, it does perform a number of functions. In addition to selecting sites for new projects or branches, managing common funds (an umbrella organization may have its own funds to be distributed to the associated projects), and supervising projects or branches in the field, the central office has the following responsibilities:

1. *Recruit and train staff*

Training starts with an orientation to the systems used in the project. After staff members receive a good theoretical grounding, they are assigned to existing branches or projects to learn the practical aspects of their jobs.

2. Act as liaison with government, donors, and sources of institutional credit

Relations with government, donors, banks, and cooperatives will be handled by the central office.

3. Monitor unit performance

A good monitoring system will provide the central office with the information it needs to determine which branches and projects are doing well and which are doing poorly. Choosing the proper indicators will "red flag" units in trouble, predict the amount of funds that need to be transferred to the units, and identify general patterns and trends.

The following indicators might be used to monitor a unit's performance:

• Total equity: cash on hand plus loans from the central office, other loans, borrower savings, and total loans outstanding minus loans overdue for more than six months.

• Number of new borrowers: does the branch or project merely serve the increasing credit needs of its old clients, or is it incorporating new borrowers?

• Portfolio quality: the ratio of the number of payments made to the number of payments due.

• Total savings: an indicator of current liquidity.

• Capital circulation: is equity primarily stockpiled cash, or is it providing loans and servicing clients?

4. Provide ongoing training for local staff

Quarterly meetings offer an opportunity for unit directors and other key staff to exchange experiences and learn more about the technical side of administering a local branch or project.

The meetings held by the ACCION staff in Colombia for the eight affiliated Colombian programs provide a useful model. Every three months, a three-day meeting is held to discuss a specific topic, such as administering the loan portfolio, training, evaluation, or selection.

5. Evaluate systems and administrative procedures to upgrade the project methodology

The methodology the project uses in its first years will evolve considerably. An important function of the central office is to continually upgrade the methodology and "package" these new insights into improved administrative procedures.

6. Provide a sense of mission and direction to the micro-credit program

This is one of the least obvious but most important functions of the central office. A good director is able to clearly define the goals of the program. This sense of mission and dedication is transmitted to the rest of those involved.

CHAPTER 8
PROGRAM MONITORING AND EVALUATION

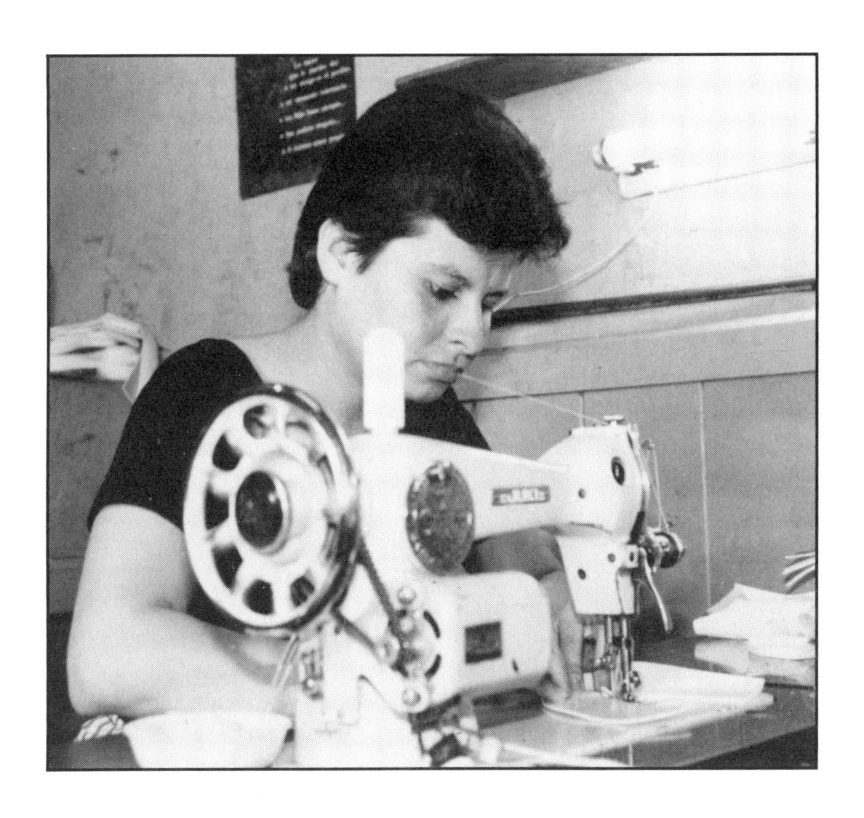

A good monitoring system will provide the program with the information it needs to determine which of the units are doing well and which are doing poorly. Choosing the proper indicators will help to "red flag" units in trouble, predict the amount of funds that need to be transferred to the branches, and identify general patterns and trends. The system used by ACCION to monitor the projects it assists is included in Appendix 1. The monitoring system should track important indicators of administrative and operational performance on a monthly basis, so that problems can be identified and dealt with promptly.

One of ACCION's objectives is to determine whether or not its projects have a measurable impact on borrowers. The program should, for example, empower and improve the living standard of minorities, women, and the poor. It should also help the smallest businesses survive, increase income, generate new employment, provide needed goods and services to the community, and focus attention on improving the community.

CASE HISTORIES

ACCION's measurement of progress in the client's businesses and in the larger community is based on its understanding of how microenterprise projects help businesses evolve. Two case histories illustrate this:

A street vendor

Before Juana Morales joined "A Better Tomorrow," she had been selling tomatoes on the ground outside the market with no protection from the sun. She had lacked working capital and every morning went to the vegetable wholesaler who advanced her tomatoes to sell that day. He said he would not charge her interest rates. However, he always gave her the worst produce at the highest price. On some days she was forced to seek out Don Gregorio, the moneylender, to borrow a few pesos for her sick child's medicine. He charged her 20% interest per week.

Two years after joining the project, Juana Morales' situation has changed. She used to make $2 per day. Now she clears $3.50. Juana knows how much she makes because she writes down what she spends and what she earns in a school exercise book. Juana works inside the market now, under a wooden stand with a corrugated tin roof that she built. Two months ago she started selling lettuce, cucumbers, and beets in addition to tomatoes and, instead of buying from the wholesaler she has used for years, she goes, with cash in hand, to wherever she can get the best produce at the best price. Last week Juana took another big step. She opened a vegetable stand in her home. Now she sells at the market in the morning and to her neighbors in the afternoon. Her savings have freed her from the moneylender and helped her to start a new business.

A micro-industry

For three years Don Luis had tried to make a go of his trouser-tailoring business, but he could not get ahead. His friends told him that the first years were the "years of struggle," and that after a while he would see his business stabilize, or even grow. "Sustained growth" was what the young lady from "Micro-Business Progress" called it.

Since he did not have much working capital, Don Luis worked hard for as long as his supply of cloth lasted and then peddled what he produced. Sometimes he sold to a store in the city, but they gave him cheques he could not cash for two months. He prayed that his battered treadle sewing machine would hold up, and he longed for the day when he could buy that electric machine his cousin was not using—the one that did the fancy stitching. With that he could really get ahead.

Encouraged by his friends, he joined "Micro-Business Progress." Two years later, "sustained growth" was within his reach.

There is no question that Don Luis is making more money—twice as much, according to his calculations. He is keeping records and, after talking to the other four members of his group, he worked out a plan for expanding his business.

Don Luis laughs when he thinks about the cramped room where he once sewed trousers. Last year he built a more spacious room with a cement floor. He gave his rickety old treadle sewing machine to his youngest son and bought his cousin's machine and another machine, as well. He also hired two new employees. Now merchants come every few days to buy what his "little factory" produces. They pay him cash. He has enough business to maintain an inventory of five bolts of cloth—a far cry from the days when he bought cloth by the yard from Dona Julia.

Is his business more "sustainable" now? It certainly seems so. He has money in the bank and a backlog of orders. He feels sure his "Modern Creations" is going to make it.

Juana Morales and Don Luis are typical of the micro-entrepreneurs that ACCION projects assist. These two examples illustrate basic indicators of business change and community impact.

A. Indicators of changes in the business

1. Profitability
Juana Morales makes $3.50 per day instead of $2. Don Luis earns "twice as much" as he did before joining the program. For micro-businesses, "increased family income" and "profitability" are generally considered to be the same, since their records are rarely sophisticated enough to measure the reinvestment of profits.

2. Improved management
Both businesses keep record books. They are not only making more money—they know they are making more money. With his friends in the credit-guarantee group, Don Luis worked out a simple plan for expanding his business. According to plan, he purchased two more machines, added a room, and now has a small but adequate inventory of cloth on hand.

3. Improved plant and equipment
Juana Morales moved from the street into the market, so that her stand now has a roof and counters. She also started to sell vegetables in her home. Don Luis has a new room for his business and two new sewing machines.

4. Changes in type and quality of production and sales
Juana sells lettuce, cucumbers, and beets in addition to the tomatoes she has always sold. Her clients seek her out because they know her vegetables are always fresh and of the highest quality. Don Luis still sells trousers, but he now uses a better grade of cloth, and the new sewing machine provides a better finish.

5. Changes in suppliers
Juana Morales buys from a variety of wholesalers; Don Luis has enough capital to purchase his cloth by the bolt at a much better price.

6. Changes in clients
Juana Morales sells to her neighbors after selling in the market. Now that "Modern Creations" produces a predictable supply of higher-quality pants, merchants come to buy from Don Luis, rather than vice versa.

7. Change in sources of credit
With their savings accounts, Juana Morales and Don Luis have increased their working capital. Juana is now free from both the moneylender and the wholesaler.

8. Dependency on the program
The businesses have progressed, but to what degree is their success dependent on close and ongoing contact with project staff? A program will have accomplished little if its businesses need help indefinitely. Juana Morales still receives program credit, but she keeps her own books and makes her own decisions. The business advisor working with Don Luis handles his books free of charge. But although Don Luis depends on that kind of help, with his increased profits he could pay for someone else to keep his books. Also, by next year Don Luis will be able to graduate from the credit program to a regular line of bank credit, thus freeing up money in the loan fund for more needy clients.

9. Sustainability
Sustainability is an estimate of how a business will fare in the future. In part, a business's financial position allows one to appraise its future viability, but the best estimate considers all aspects of the enterprise's well-being. To determine the business's ability to sustain itself, one asks how far it has evolved from the "years of struggle" to "stability" and on to "sustained growth."

B. Indicators of community impact
The case histories also illustrate the impact of micro-enterprise projects on the community. Various changes tend to occur:

1. Increased income
The businesses register increased profits, which translate into increased income for the owners' families.

2. Increased employment
Employment generation starts by changing part-time into full-time work. Juana Morales now sells vegetables in her home in addition to selling in the market, and she works an extra three hours per day. Her vegetable stand did not create any new jobs, which is typical of loans to micro-commerces. Don Luis, as a manufacturer, gave jobs to his son and a neighbor.

3. Training
It is important not only to track the new jobs that have been created, but also to consider the skills learned by those who work there. Don

Luis's son and his young neighbor were unemployed before they began to work for "Modern Creations." Within a year after starting, they had become trained tailors—a skill that could eventually enable them to set up their own tailoring shops.

4. Increased availability of goods and services in the community
Juana's new business now provides vegetables in the neighborhood. The expansion of Don Luis's business did not have a comparable effect because the supply of trousers in the community had already been sufficient.

5. New links with other local businesses
Juana Morales now sells merchandise to her neighbors and buys from a new wholesaler. Don Luis subcontracts some of his orders for trousers to other tailors in the community when he has a backlog of orders.

6. Displacement
A negative community impact of business expansion is displacement, whereby the improved businesses drive out other established businesses.

In the large urban market where Juana Morales works, new immigrants have been pouring into the area. Because demand has been expanding continually, many new businesses are created. Don Luis believes that economic conditions in his community have improved and that with more prosperity, people have begun to dress better. All the tailoring shops are still in business, and he contracts local tailors to help him meet the demand.

7. Increasing prosperity through the "multiplier effect"

"Displacement" may be canceled out by the "multiplier effect." When the poor earn more, they consume from other local businesses. Juana Morales can now buy her children two pairs of shoes per year from the local cobbler, and she can afford school uniforms for all her children. Since she earns more, her family eats better—she purchases meat from the woman a few stalls away and more rice and beans from another member of her credit-guarantee group. The owners of these businesses, in turn, have increased their incomes and their purchases.

C. Evaluating project impact

A simple procedure built into the normal system of credit-application and renewal can help determine the impact of the project at little additional cost. The key to making the evaluation useful is to integrate it into the decision-making process. While all information is "interesting," every piece of data collected has its cost. The more complex the monitoring, the less likely it will be kept up to date and the less likely the staff (who may be busy with the day-to-day operation of the project) will use it.

The ideal evaluation is simple and practical. And if all the regional offices use the same system, the results can be easily compared.

The evaluation measures the following:

1. Borrowers' personal attributes

These include age, sex, years of experience as a business owner, educational level, status in the household, number of dependents, and family income.

2. Characteristics of the businesses and changes encouraged by the program

Characteristics of the existing businesses include net business income (sales less costs), the number of permanent and full-time employees, and their wages. Changes in the businesses include, for example, whether the owners are now using a bookkeeping system, have made improvements in the place of business (a new sign, new building, new coat of paint, etc.); have purchased equipment or tools, have begun to sell or produce new products, have started a new business or closed the previous one.

3. Level of participation in the program
The evaluator determines whether the borrowers have remained active in the program by asking them if they have helped in the formation of new groups (or recruited others), if they actively participate in the training meetings and other special activities of the program, and if they prefer to receive their loans individually or through the group mechanism.

4. Degree of solidarity and mutual assistance
The evaluation indicates whether the group members have been providing one another with advice and information, if they collectively make purchases of merchandise and raw materials, and if they have set up a cooperative business.

By analyzing this information, the staff should have a clearer idea of the program's impact. Of course, each of these themes—the generation of employment or changes in the relationship between businesses—could be studied in more depth. This simple system does not replace in-depth studies. It simply serves to monitor the process of change and the impact of the program.

D. Evaluation study

The design of the evaluation study is based on the assumption that as clients continue to participate in the project, their businesses will continue to evolve and grow. To measure this development, the study collects information as participants enter the project, after six months, and again after eighteen months of participation. Information from the original application for credit provides a base line. Additional information is collected at the time of credit renewal. As the program grows, it periodically becomes necessary to select a sample of clients for evaluation. The sample should be chosen randomly and divided according to the type of economic activity.

ACCION has prepared a detailed guide of evaluation procedures known as the "Evaluation Manual." It is currently available to the public.

Chapter 9
Board Development
and Public Relations

BOARD DEVELOPMENT

ACCION's experience has shown that a wide variety of organizations—cooperatives, non-profit groups, community associations and even financial institutions—can effectively administrate a micro enterprise support program. In most of these instances the board of directors functions as a governing body whose specific responsibilities and functions will vary, depending on the structure of the administrative agency and its objectives. It is necessary to have an active board to ensure the continuity and stability of the program.

In general, board functions and responsibilities are as follows:

A. Legal representation
The board of directors is legally responsible to public authorities for compliance with legal and fiscal requirements. The board delegates authority to the executive director and other executive officers on behalf of the organization.

B. Setting general policies
The board sets policies and general objectives for the organization. A weakness of many boards is their confusion between the setting of general policies and the actual management of the organization. The proper role of the board is to establish policy and allow the executive director to manage the organization.

C. Financial supervision
The board should assume responsibility for the financial welfare of the organization by establishing general fiscal policies and periodically reviewing financial statements.

D. Supervision of management
The board authorizes the executive director to manage the program according to their general policies. The board should also set up an evaluation system for reviewing the director's performance.

E. Raising funds and resources
An important function of the board in a non-profit organization is active participation in fund-raising. This involves submitting proposals at the national and international level, calling on potential donors, organizing and taking part in special fund-raising events, and direct personal financial support of the organization. As part of a corporation, or even a non-profit foundation, the board will be active in obtaining other sources

of funds, such as lines of commercial credit, investments, or fund guarantees.

F. Institutional and government liaison
Board members should establish channels of communication and cooperation with other organizations related to the program and, whenever necessary, with government authorities. This kind of networking, either formal or informal, helps publicize the organization and ensures its political independence. At the same time it offers the program and its beneficiaries access to the centers of power, in both the private and public sectors.

G. Public relations and education
Programs should be active in public relations and education. The board members can play a leading role in these areas by using their contacts and influence to ensure that local authorities are sensitive to informal-sector development strategies.

The nature of the board of directors will vary according to the relationship of the micro-business program to the administrative organization. If an organization is created exclusively to administer the micro-business program, then it is important that the board members share program goals and understand and support the methodology of the program. When an existing organization decides to expand its services to include a micro-business program, it is possible that the functioning board of directors may not be well informed about strategies for assisting micro-businesses. In this case, it will be necessary either to appoint additional board members who will actively support the program, or set up a committee within the board to assume responsibility for the program's management.

Finally, in the case of cooperatives or community groups where the board is made up of program beneficiaries, it is best to form an advisory council of local leaders who would be willing to help the organization set up the necessary connections, carry on public relations, and perform fund-raising duties.

PUBLIC RELATIONS AND RESOURCE DEVELOPMENT

As the program and organization grow, a department should be created to oversee public relations and resource-development activities. If many small organizations operate micro-business programs in close proximity to each other, it is usually impractical for each to create such a department. In Colombia, small independent organizations combined resources and formed an association specifically for resource development and public-relations activities.

A. Objectives
Resource development and public relations should be structured around three sets of objectives:

1. Financial self-suffiency
A department created for resource development and public relations contributes to the organization's objective of achieving financial self-sufficiency. In order to maintain a solid financial base, the program must develop a network of diversified financial support, at both the domestic and international levels. Even when a program can cover its operating expenses by program-generated income, there will always be a need for additional resources to develop new projects and ideas.

2. Promoting the importance of the informal sector

It is essential that local public and private leaders understand the significance of the informal sector and of micro-business development strategies. Statistics on a program's impact can be of interest to national policy makers and should be presented in terms that are understood by the public (e.g., the number of jobs created).

3. Supporting initiatives in private development

In most countries, there is no tradition of financial support for private-development initiatives. This tradition should be developed.

B. Responsibilities

While a department of public relations and resource development may pursue the general objectives in various ways, it should define its specific responsibilities along the following guidelines:

1. Identification of potential domestic and international funding

Foundations, corporations, and individuals can be contacted by letter, sent written proposals, and educated through special events.

2. Contact with the news media

Contacting individual reporters in the press, radio, and television is a good way of informing the public about the program.

3. Organization of special events

The department can use special events to inform key sectors of the public and solicit donations for the program.

4. Production of educational materials

The department should publish pamphlets, annual reports, audio-visual aids, and other educational materials. The use of audio-visual aids is an especially attractive and effective method of promoting the program.

CHAPTER 10
FINANCIAL REPORTING AND MONITORING

Three reports are necessary for effective management of the program. They not only inform donors and other interested persons about the nature and status of the project, but also help the board of directors evaluate the program.

A. Monthly statistical report

A brief report should be produced every month, summarizing basic program indicators, such as the number of new participants, amounts loaned and recovered, average value of loans, types of participants, etc. Most of the information in this report can be found in the loan applications filled out by prospective participants. The statistical report is useful in evaluating the program's achievements. To enable inter-project comparisons, ACCION has standardized the form of this report for twenty-two affiliated programs. A sample report and an explanation and definition of its indicators can be found in Appendix 1.

B. Financial report

Every program must produce financial reports on a quarterly basis. These reports should include a statement of income and expenses and a general balance sheet in accordance with standard accounting principles. If the micro-enterprise credit program is the sole activity of the organization, such statements would represent the financial status of the entire organization. If the program is a division within an organization handling other programs, it is essential that quarterly financial reports reflect the status of only the micro-enterprise credit program.

Within the scope of its financial reports, the program should establish clear and consistent policies for defining when a loan is in default and when a default loan is counted as a loss. In addition, the program should have provisions for a reserve fund against losses. The format for financial reports of micro-enterprise programs, with instructions for use, is included in Appendix 2.

C. Auditing

It is imperative that every program contract a reputable auditing firm to carry out financial audits. An external audit assures investors that the program is following standard accounting practices. It allows the managers to detect problems and errors in the accounting system and financial administration of the organization. Making use of a reputable firm also assures the board of directors that the organization, for which they are legally responsible, is in good order.

APPENDIX 1
MONTHLY STATISTICAL REPORT

APPENDIX 1

MONTHLY STATISTICAL REPORT

Program _____

Month _____

Exchange rate U.S.$ _____

	INDIVIDUAL	SOLIDARITY GROUPS	
	Micro-producers	Micro-producers	Micro-vendors
1. No. of *new* enterprises/ groups financed			
2. No. of loans disbursed			
3. Amount of loans disbursed			
4. Average loan value			
5. No. of loans recovered			
6. Amount of loans recovered (principal)			
7. New participants			
– Men	/ %	/ %	/ %
– Women	/ %	/ %	/ %
8. Current client savings			
9. Cost per unit loaned			
10. Loans refinanced			
11. Default rate			
12. Active loan portfolio			
13. Interest and fees (income)			
14. Administrative, operational, and financial program costs			
15. Courses and meetings/ participants			

Explanation of line items

1. The number of enterprises or groups that received a loan for the first time this month.
2. Total number of loans disbursed during the month.
3. The dollar value of the loans in number 2 above.
4. Number 3 divided by number 2.
5. The number of loans repaid in full during the month.
6. The amount of principal recovered in the month.
7. Only new clients who joined the program in the month.
8. The amount of current client savings.
9. The cost per unit loaned is derived by dividing the *total* monthly program costs by the amount loaned during the month.
   (Monthly costs include salaries and benefits, expenses for materials, transportation, communication, and all other operational expenses, as well as professional services and technical assistance from ACCION.)
10. The number and amount of loans that are refinanced during the current month.
11. The default rate is calculated by:

    $$\frac{\text{amount of principal in default} \times 100}{\text{amount of principal in the active loan portfolio}}$$

12. The active loan portfolio equals the amount of principal loaned minus the amount of principal recovered.
13. All income from interest and fees.
14. Monthly program costs (see number 9).
15. The type of meeting or course and the number of participants.

APPENDIX 2
FORMAT FOR PROGRAM FINANCIAL REPORTS

Instructions for the preparation of Form II "Financial Statement"

General Instructions

The FORM II spreadsheets contain four pages and include the following sections:

Page 1—Balance Sheet
Page 2—Contribution to Net Worth Statement
       (Profit and Loss Statement)
       Financial Summary
Page 3—Reconciliation of Net Worth
       Reconciliation of Loan Portfolio
Page 4—Schedule 1—Banking Relations
       Schedule 2—Medium/Long-Term Debt Structure
       Schedule 3—Loan-Portfolio Analysis

Preparation of the financial statement should be based on closing figures, preferably month-end amounts. The balance sheet provides static analysis of "one moment in time," and the statement of contribution to net worth (profit and loss) reviews performance over a period of time.

Many institutions that provide micro-lending programs to their communities engage in other activities totally unrelated to micro-lending or the ACCION/AITEC programs. For this reason, when the initial spreadsheet is prepared for each foundation, the financial statement is thoroughly analyzed so that only those items pertaining to the micro-lending activity are allocated on the ACCION/AITEC spreadsheet.

It may be advisable to seek the advice of an accountant when reallocating financial-statement items. The guiding rule is that "only micro-lending activities and related overhead items are to be included on the ACCION/AITEC spreadsheets." To assure consistency in the reporting process, the guidelines used for allocating line items must be adhered to in subsequent spreadsheets.

In general, completing the spreadsheet is done in three stages:

STAGE 1 Completion of Page 4 (auxiliary schedules). Certain information from these schedules will be transferred directly to specific lines on the other pages.

STAGE 2 Completion of Pages 1 and 2 (Balance Sheet, Contribution to Net Worth Statement, and Financial Summary).

STAGE 3 Completion of Page 3 (reconciliations). This page need not be completed when a micro-lending institution's figures are placed on a spreadsheet for the first time.

Specific Instructions

STAGE 1/PAGE 4

I. *Schedule 1 = Banking Relations/Short-Term Debt*

   A. *Column A*—List the names of all banks that provide either deposit services or short-term credit lines. if a bank provides credit lines to a micro-lending program but the lines are not utilized as of the statement date, the bank must still be listed under Column A.

B. *Column B = Sight/Demand Deposits*—List all (black) balances available to the micro-lending institutions on a *sight or demand* basis at each bank. Savings accounts, money market accounts, and any interest-bearing accounts that are available on demand should also be included under Column B.

Any overdraft (red) balances should *not* be listed in Column B, but under Column F.

C. *Column C = Certificates of Deposit Time Deposits*—List the total of all deposits available to the micro-lending institution at each bank on a time- or fixed-contract basis (not readily available on demand). This caption will normally also include any guarantee or escrow deposits.

D. *Column D = Total Short-Term Credit Lines*—List the total of *credit lines* available to the institution at each bank regardless of whether the lines are utilized or not.

E. *Column E = Total Outstanding, Loans and Overdrafts*—List total *outstanding* amounts due to each bank under existing credit lines as of the statement date. Any overdrafts should be included in this column.

F. *Column F = Unused Credit Lines*—Entries for this column should be obtained by subtracting the entry for Column E from the entry for Column D. It represents the incremental borrowing potential that is readily available to the micro-lending institutions at each bank.

Once the schedule has been completed, Columns B through E should be totaled. (The totals for Columns B, C, and E will later be transferred to lines 2, 3, and 28 respectively on Page 1 of the spreadsheet.)

II. *Schedule 2 = Medium/Long-Term Debt Structure*

This schedule will help distinguish concessionary and non-concessionary debt.

Concessionary debt is all debt acquired by the institution on terms that are clearly more favorable than those provided under a traditional commercial or banking transaction. Typically, concesssionary debt may be available from certain international organizations such as A.I.D., the I.D.B., and certain European and Canadian government agencies.

Non-concessionary medium- and long-term debt can be defined as all debt that is not considered "concessionary."

A. *Column A = Lender*—List the name of each "concessionary" lender in the spaces provided in the upper section of the schedule. List the name of each "non-concessionary" lender in the lower section of the schedule. If one lender has made two or more loans to the institution, each loan should be listed on a separate line.

B. *Column B = Total Outstandings*—List the total principal amount outstanding as of the statement date, under loans granted by each lender. *Do not* include any interest that may be payable.

C. *Column C = Principal Amounts Due Within One Year*—List the total of *principal* payments that must be made under the loans during the 360-day period after the statement date. *Do not* include any interest that may be payable.

D. *Column D = Principal Amounts Due in Later Years*—List the total of principal payments that must be made under the loans during the period following *360 days after* the statement date. Do *not* include any interest that may be payable. Entries under this column *must* be equal to the entry for Column B less the entry for Column C.

E. *Column E* = Indicate the final maturity date of each loan.

Add up all entries for concessionary debt in Columns B, C, and D and make sub-total entries in the spaces provided.

Add up all entries for non-concessionary debt in Columns B, C, and D and make sub-total entries in the spaces provided.

Finally, add the two sub-total amounts in Columns B, C, and D and make total entries in the spaces provided. (The sub-total entries in Column C will later be transferred to lines 32 and 31 on Page 1, and the sub-total entries in Column D will be transferred to lines 46 and 38 on Page 1.)

III. *Schedule 3 = Loan Portfolio Analysis*

This schedule is self-explanatory. The entire loan portfolio must be divided into Solidarios and Micro-Empresarios. Within each of these categories, a breakdown will be provided between loans that are current, refinanced, and past due. (Any loan with one payment past due is to be considered past due in its entirety!)

Finally, at the bottom of Schedule 3 there is a request for information regarding unrecovered loans that have been written off. Although these loans are considered unrecoverable, a record of them should always be maintained.

STAGE 2/PAGES 1 AND 2

I. Instructions for Completing Page 1 = Balance Sheet

A. *Current Assets*—Cash and other assets such as temporary investments in securities, accounts and notes receivable, inventory, supplies, and prepayments that presumably will be converted into cash, will be used, or will expire during the normal one-year operating cycle.

LINE:
1. *Petty Cash* — Bills and coin on hand and money that may be available on the premises either in a small vault or in a coin safe.
2. *Cash in Banks* — From Page 4, Schedule 1, Column B.
3. *Other Deposits* — From Page 4, Schedule 1, Column C.
4. *Total Cash* — The sum of lines 1 through 3.
5. *Other Accounts Receivable* — List any other miscellaneous accounts receivable that are collectible or convertible into cash within the next 360-day period.
7. *Loan Portfolio* — From Page 4, Schedule 3.
8. *Less: Reserve for Loan Losses* — The amount allocated as a reserve for bad debts or loan losses.
9. *Net Loans* — Line 7 minus Line 8.
12. *Inventories and Other Current Assets* — List any other miscellaneous inventories or current assets that are an integral part of the foundation's micro-lending business.
15. *Total Current Assets* — The sum of lines 4 through 14.
17. *Other Investments* — List all other investments in stock or equities that are not easily liquidated on a short-term basis.
18. *Furniture/Equipment* — List all furniture and equipment that is used as an integral part of the micro-lending activity.
19. *Vehicles* — List net depreciated value of any vehicles that are used in the micro-lending business.
20. *Net Real Estate Owned* — List any ownership of real estate that is used in the micro-lending business net of any mortgages owed on the property.
25. *Total Assets* — The sum of lines 16 through 25.

B. *Liabilities*—
LINE:
26. *Accounts Payable* — List any accounts payable that are due within the next 360-day period and are related to the micro-lending business.
28. *Short-Term Debt = Banks* — From Page 4, Schedule 1, Column E.
29. *Short-Term Debt = Others* — List any other short-term debt that may be payable within the next 360-day period.
31. *Current Portion of Long-Term Debt = Concessionary* — From Page 4, Schedule 2.
32. *Current Portion of Long-Term Debt = Non-Concessionary*—From Page 4, Schedule 2.
37. *Total Current Liabilities* — The sum of lines 26 through 36.

38. *Medium/Long-Term Debt = Non-Concessionary* — From Page 4, Schedule 2.
43. *Total Medium/Long-Term Debt* — The sum of lines 38 through 42.
45. *Total Non-Concessionary Debt* — Line 43 plus line 44.
46. *Concessionary Debt (Quasi-Equity)* — From Page 4, Schedule 2.
47. *Total Liabilities* — The sum of lines 37, 45, and 46.

C. *Net Worth*—
LINE:
48. *Net Worth*—Line 25 minus line 47.
49. *Total Capitalization*—Line 46 plus line 48.
50. *Total Liabilities Plus Net Worth*—Line 47 plus line 48. This amount must be equal to the amount on line 25.

II. *Instructions for Completing Page 2 = Contribution to Net Worth Statement (Profit and Loss)*

Indicates the number of months of operation included in the statement and the ending date of the contribution to the net worth statement. The ending date should coincide with the closing date of the balance sheet.

A. *Instructions for Completing Contribution to Net Worth Statement*
LINE:
51. *Interest Collected on Loans*—The total amount of interest that has been collected on loans since the beginning of the period.
52. *Fees Collected on Loans*—The total amount of loan-related fees that has been collected on loans since the beginning of the period.
54. *Total Funds Revenue*—The sum of lines 51 through 53.
55. *Interest Expense = Banks*—The total amount of interest paid to banks during the period.
56. *Interest Expense = Concessionary Debt*—The total amount of interest paid to international organizations and others on concessionary debt.
57. *Loan Related Fees*—The total amount of commitment fees, commissions and other loan-related fees paid to lending organizations. Do not include fees paid to ACCION/AITEC.
58. *ACCION/AITEC Fees*—The total amount of fees paid to ACCION/AITEC during the period.
60. *Total Funds Cost*—The sum of lines 55 through 59.
61. *Net Revenue From Funds*—Line 54 minus line 60.
62. *Plus: Other Miscellaneous Income*—Include any other miscellaneous income that is not related to revenue from funds.
64. *Less: Staff Payments/Salaries*—Include all payments made for salaries, social security, fringes, bonuses, and any other payments to the staff, including upper management.

65. *Premises Expenses*—Include all payments made during the period either as building-lease expense, maintenance of the office building where the institution operates, or as other expenses related to leasing the offices of the micro-lending institutions.
66. *Other Operating Expenses*—List all other operating expenses of the institution that are related to the micro-lending business.
69. *Gross Income*—Line 61 plus line 62 less lines 64 through 68.
70. *Less: Provision for Loan Losses*—The amount that has been provided for loan losses or bad debts during the past period.
72. *Plus: Extraordinary Recovery of Loans Previously Written Off*—The total of all amounts recovered during the period which had been previously written off.
75. *Contribution to Net Worth (Net Income)*—Line 69 minus lines 70 through 71 plus lines 72 and 74.

B. *Instructions for Completion of Financial Summary*
LINE:
76. *Total Funds Revenue*—Copy from line 54, above.
77. *Contribution to Net Worth (Net Income)*—Copy from line 75, above.
78. *Net Margin*—Line 77 divided by line 76 multiplied by 100.
79. *Return on Net Worth*—Line 77 divided by line 48 multiplied by the fraction 12 over the number of months in the period being reported. Multiply by 100.
81. *Return on Total Capitalization*—Line 77 divided by line 49 multiplied by the fraction 12 over the number of months in the period being reported. Multiply by 100.
82. *Total Cash and Unused Bank Lines*—Line 4 plus the total of unused bank lines taken from Page 4, Schedule 1, Column F.
83. *Total Cash and Unused Bank Lines = Current Liabilities*—Line 82 divided by line 37.
84. *Current Ratio*—Line 15 divided by line 37.
86. *Total Debt = Net Worth (Debt/Equity ratio)*—Line 47 divided by line 48.
87. *Total Debt Less Quasi-Equity = Total Capitalization (Debt to Capitalization ratio)*—Line 45 divided by line 49.

STAGE 3/PAGE 3

I. *Instructions for Completing Reconciliation of Net Worth*
LINE:
89. *Opening Net Worth*—Enter the ending net worth (line 48) as of the end of the previous reporting period.
90. *Plus: Current Period Contribution to Net Worth*—Copy amount entered on line 75.

91. *Sale of Equity*—Enter the amount of any new capital contributions or additional equity contributed to the institution during the period.
92. *Donations Received*—Enter the amount of any donations or grants received by the foundation during the period.
95. *Total Additions*—The sum of lines 90 through 94.
96. *Less: Dividends*—Enter the amount of any dividends (if any) paid to stockholders during the reporting period.
97. *Less: Other Distributions (specify)*—Enter the amount of any other distributions or reductions of capital paid out by the institution during the reporting period.
99. *Total Deductions*—The sum of lines 96 through 98.
100. *Increase (Decrease) in Net Worth*—Line 95 minus line 99.
101. *Ending Net Worth*—Line 89 plus line 100. This line must be equal to the amount on line 48.

II. *Instructions for Completing Reconciliation of Loan Portfolio*
LINE:
102. *Opening Total Loans (from Prior Period)*—Enter the amount of total loans from the end of the prior reporting period (line 7 from the spreadsheet of the prior reporting period).
103. *Plus: New Loans Disbursed*—Enter the total principal amount of new loans disbursed during the reporting period.
104. *Less: Principal Amounts Collected*—Enter the total of the principal amounts collected during the reporting period.
105. *Less: Loans Written Off*—Enter the total amount of loans written off during the reporting period.
106. *Less: Ending Total Loans*—Line 102 plus line 103 minus the sum of lines 104 and 105.

III. *Instructions for Completing Reserve for Loan Losses*
LINE:
107. *Opening Loan-Loss Reserve (from Prior Period)*—Enter the amount of the loan-loss reserve as of the end of the prior reporting period (line 8 from the spreadsheet of the prior reporting period).
108. *Plus: Provision for Loan Losses*—Copy the amount from line 70.
109. *Less: Loans Written Off*—Copy the amount entered previously on line 105 (the total amount of loans written off during the reporting period).
110. *Ending Loan Loss Reserve*—Line 107 plus line 108 minus line 109.
111. *Net Loans*—Line 106 minus line 110. This amount must be equal to the amount on line 9.

Form II Financial Statement   Page 1

Name and Address of Organization: Currency: ....
....   Auditors: ....
....   Approved by: ....
....   Executive Director

BALANCE SHEET Date: /   /
ASSETS	LIABILITIES

1. Petty cash	......	26. Accounts payable	......
2. Cash in banks (Sch 1)	......	27.	......
3. Other deposits (CD/Time)	......	28. Short-term debt — banks	......
4. Total cash	......	29. Short-term debt — others	......
5. Misc. other A/C Rec. (Collectible within 360 days)	......	30.	......
6.	......	31. Current portion of long-term concessionary	......
7. Loan portfolio	......	32. Current portion of long-term non-concessionary	......
8. Less: reserve for loan losses	......	33.	......
9. Net loans	......	34.	......
10.	......	35.	......
11.	......	36.	......
12. Inventories and other current assets	......	37. Total current liabilities	......
13.	......	38. Medium/long-term debt non-concessionary	......
14.	......	39.	......
15. Total current assets	......	40.	......
16.	......	41.	......
17. Other investments	......	42.	......
18. Furniture/equipment	......	43. Total medium/long-term debt	......
19. Vehicles	......	44. Other	......
20. Net real-estate owned	......	45. Total non-concessionary debt	......
21.	......	46. Concessionary debt (quasi-equity)	......
22.	......	47. Total liabilities	......
23.	......	48. Net worth	......
24.	......	49. Total capitalization	......
25. Total assets	......	50. Total liabilities plus net worth	......

Page 2

CONTRIBUTION TO NET WORTH STATEMENT
(PROFIT AND LOSS)
____ MONTHS ENDING ____/____/____

51. Interest collected on loans ....
52. Fees collected on loans ....
53.
54.   TOTAL FUNDS REVENUE ....
55. Interest expense — banks ....
56. Interest expense — concessionary debt ....
57. Loan-related fees ....
58. ACCION/AITEC fees ....
59. ....
60.   TOTAL FUNDS COST ....
61.   NET REVENUE FROM FUNDS ....
62. Plus: other miscellaneous income ....
63.
64. Less: Staff payments/salaries ....
65.   Premises expenses ....
66.   Other operating expenses ....
67. ....
68. ....
69.   GROSS INCOME ....
70. Less: Provision for loan losses ....
71.
72. Plus: Extraordinary recovery of loans previously written off ....
73.
74.
75.   CONTRIBUTION TO NET WORTH (NET INCOME) ....

FINANCIAL SUMMARY

PROFITABILITY

    76. TOTAL FUNDS REVENUE ....
    77. CONTRIBUTION TO NET WORTH (NET INCOME) ....
    78. NET MARGIN % ....
    79. RETURN ON NET WORTH % ....
    80. ....
    81. RETURN ON TOTAL CAPITALIZATION % ....

LIQUIDITY

    82. TOTAL CASH AND UNUSED BANK LINES OF CREDIT ....
    83. TOTAL CASH AND UNUSED BANK LINES OF CREDIT CURRENT LIABILITIES ....
    84. CURRENT RATIO (CURRENT ASSETS/ LIABILITIES) ....
    85.

continued ...

CAPITAL

86. TOTAL DEBT — NET WORTH ....
87. TOTAL DEBT LESS QUASI-EQUITY — TOTAL
    CAPITALIZATION ....
88.

RECONCILIATION OF NET WORTH
Date: __/__/__ **Page 3**

89. OPENING NET WORTH (from prior period) ....
90. Plus: Current period contribution to net worth ....
91.   Sale of equity ....
92.   Donations received ....
93.   Others (specify) ....
94. ....
95. TOTAL ADDITIONS ....
96. Less: Dividends ....
97.   Other distributions (specify) ....
98. ....
99. TOTAL DEDUCTIONS ....
100. Increase (decrease) in net worth ....
101. ENDING NET WORTH ....

RECONCILIATION OF LOAN PORTFOLIO

102. Opening total loans (from prior period) ....
103. Plus: new loans disbursed ....
104. Less: Principal amounts collected ....
105.   Loans written off ....
106.   Ending total loans ....

Reserve for loan losses

107. Opening loan-loss reserve (from prior period) ....
108. Plus: provision for loan losses (current period) ....
109. Less: loans written off ....
110. Ending loan loss reserve ....
111. NET LOANS ....

Date: ___/___/___ **Page 4**

SCHEDULE 1 — BANKING RELATIONS/SHORT-TERM DEBT

A	B	C	D	E	F
	\multicolumn{2}{c}{Deposits}	\multicolumn{3}{c}{Credit Lines}
Name of Bank	Sight/ Demand	CD's/ Time	Total ST Credit Lines	Outstanding Loans/ Overdrafts	Unused Lines
TOTAL:	(2)	(3)		(28)	

SCHEDULE 2 — MEDIUM/LONG-TERM DEBT STRUCTURE

A	B	C	D	E
Lender Concessionary	Total O/S	Principal Amt. Due w/l yr.	Principal Amt. Due in later years	Final Maturity
SUB-TOTAL:		(31)	(46)	
Non-Concessionary				
SUB-TOTAL:		(32)	(38)	
TOTALS:				

continued . . .

SCHEDULE 3 — LOAN PORTFOLIO ANALYSIS

	Solidarios #	Solidarios $	Micro-Empresarios #	Micro-Empresarios $	Total #	Total $
CURRENT						
REFINANCED						
PAST DUE						
TOTAL						(5)
MEMO A/C						
LOANS WRITTEN OFF						